Personal Finance and Inv

Playbook

Take Control of Your Future with 13 Surprising (Yet Proven) Strategies to Get Out of Debt, Master Productivity and Make Money From Home in 2019

By

Steve E. Carruso

&

Financial Freedom Blueprint

I am not a financial advisor, this is not financial advice. This is not an investment guide nor investment advice. I am not recommending you buy any of the stocks listed here. Any form of investment or trading is liable to lose you money.

This ebook contains "forward-looking"statements as that term is defined in Section 27A of the Securities Act and Section 21E of the Securities Exchange Act of 1934, as amended by the Private Securities Litigation Reform Act of 1995. All statements, other than historical facts are forward-looking statements.

Forward-looking statements concern future circumstances and results and other statements that are not historical facts and are sometimes identified by the words "may," "will," "should," "potential," "intend," "expect," "endeavor," "seek," "anticipate," "estimate," "overestimate," "underestimate," "believe," "could," "project," "predict," "continue," "target" or other similar words or expressions. Forward-looking statements are based upon current plans, estimates and expectations that are subject to risks, uncertainties and assumptions. Should one or more of these risks or uncertainties materialize, or should underlying assumptions prove incorrect, actual results may vary materially from those indicated or anticipated by such forward-looking statements. The inclusion of such statements should not be regarded as a representation that such plans, estimates or expectations will be achieved

Table Of Contents

Financial Freedom at Any Age

A Proven Plan to Save Money & Achieve Debt Free Living... Even If You're Drowning in Debt Right Now - Plus No Spend Challenge Tips & Passive Income Investing Strategies

By

Steve E. Carruso

Introduction

Debt is scary, and thoughts of overcoming it often feel overwhelming. However, according to the Pew Charitable Trust, about 80% of American households are in debt. But it is not just the households! Businesses and even countries have been caught up in a cycle of borrowing and spending that keeps increasing their loads[1]. Instead of concentrating on clearing the current debts, many simply jump to another line of credit to borrow more.

Many people getting into debt appear not to understand the effect it will have on their lives. However, it is not your fault. That is right. The reality of debt is that life in America is tough and living without borrowing can be really tough. Many people cannot afford to pay for higher education, a mortgage, or even vacations directly from their pockets. So, they resort to loans that also appear relatively easy to get but sink them further into debt.

When you finally realize the debt burden on your shoulder, the following key questions start running through your mind:

- "How did I get here?"
- "Am I really normal with this heavy debt burden?"
- "Is it okay to be in debt?"
- "Is my life completely damaged?"
- "Is there a way out?"

Even before digging deeper into how people slip into the problem of debt, it is prudent to know that the journey to financial freedom is possible. Though you are in debt, it can be cleared, and you will be okay!

You only need to understand how to navigate through debt and use this two-part book to overcome it. This guide provides actionable strategies and insights that you can apply in life to make clearing debt easy, gradual, and fun. Indeed, the process does not end there. This book helps you continue with the journey to financial freedom. Many people have overcome debts and marched to financial freedom. So can you.

[1] Megan, E, 2017, *15 Scary Facts about Debt that Should Alarm you*. <available at> https://www.cheatsheet.com/money-career/facts-about-debt-may-alarm-you-today.html/

The Debt Problem: Why you are stuck

While getting into debt appears so simple, trying to get out looks impossible for many people. You might have tried to skip meals or even sold a car to clear off the debt. But, the problem recurred in a bigger magnitude after a couple of years. While some keep saying that it is impossible to live without debt, this book will demonstrate that it is possible to overcome debt and enjoy a debt-free lifestyle.

When you are told that living with debt is normal, it is not true because there are people who have succeeded in addressing their debts and attained financial freedom. This is why this book was created. Here are some things that often make debts look too complex to address:

- **Many Conventional Pieces of Advice are Useless:** If you look at the common methods recommended for addressing debts out there, they are ineffective. Some financial experts out there will write solutions that are simply aimed at helping them drive traffic to their sites as opposed to getting you out of the gutter.

Instead of using any method suggested out there, the right thing is sticking with tested and proven strategies. For example, a strategy that simply requires you to just start making payments will only work in the short-term. Instead, it is important to use workable solutions outlined in this book. The strategies outlined here have been used with great results by people who initially thought that getting out of debt was impossible. This book focuses on empowering you to note the debt problem, understand it, clear it, and finally achieve financial freedom.

- **The figures make the debts look too large.** After taking several loans, such as a student loan and a mortgage, a total debt that runs into thousands of dollars might look humongous. In such a scenario, you are left wondering: "Where do I start addressing the problem?" Unfortunately, this is the wrong approach to take if you want to clear debts.

The proper way to do it is by creating the right mindset. Once you develop the commitment and desire to clear the debt, it will become easy to seek professional help and motivation. However small or big the debt might be, you can clear it with the right motivation.

- **The period required to clear debts appears too long.** When you are applying for a loan, it is common to get fixated on the thing you want to achieve. For example, couples are overjoyed when their mortgage is approved. However, it later dawns on them that they will need to continuously repay the loan for more than 15 years.

Thoughts of hundreds of months trying to clear a debt can appear scary. That said, this should not worry you. The good thing with long-term loans is that only a small amount of your income goes into clearing it. Therefore, it should not scare you. Instead, the long period should motivate you to stick to the repayment schedule.

If you find it hard to stick to the payments, this book will demonstrate how you can stay on top of your debts and personal financial operations through automation. This involves using applications that help with budgeting and even sending reminders so that you can make all payments on time.

- **Poor Planning:** If you do not have the right debt repayment plan, it will be very difficult to get out of debt. Poor planning will make it easy for you to slide back into debts even before getting out. This book helps you to look at your debt broadly and craft a winning recovery strategy.

For example, you should ensure you have an emergency fund and use this book to craft a reliable plan. You are also encouraged to cut unnecessary costs and direct the funds towards clearing your debt.

What this Book is about

When you look at the statistics about people with debts, it is scary. Indeed, a closer look at the route to your current stressful debt status could make clearing it to look difficult. However, you will be surprised to realize that it can be rather simple and fast.

No matter how much debt you have, even if it is more than $100,000, you can topple it. You are not hopeless and you are not bad. You are a normal human being. You can overcome the debt.

This book provides you with actionable steps that you can use to craft the right financial behavior, cut unnecessary spending, and become that dream financial icon you always dreamt of. This book pools tested and proven strategies that you will find easy to apply, associate with, and embark on the journey to a debt free life.

The book is broken into two key parts that seek to get you out of debt and further blast you to financial freedom.

Part One: Paying Off Your Debt

This is a comprehensive evaluation of the current debt problem and how it can be eliminated.

- This part is carefully constructed to help you understand the current debt problem and why it is possible to overcome it. It explains that being in debt has become a common thing because everybody- parents, sisters, brothers, and even institutions- appears to be in debt. It demonstrates that you cannot simply wallow in debt wondering why it grew into thousands of dollars in the first place.
- To address the debt, you will have to develop the right mindset and craft a winning formula. However, you do not need to change your lifestyle. You will only need to make some adjustments and adopt initiatives such as No Spend days or weeks to raise funds to clear the debt.
- Clearing debt is not a punishment. Though you have been in debt, credit cards have a lot of penalties, and your credit score is very poor, these are not reasons to make debt clearance harsh. This part is created on the premise that you can plan to clear debt and still have a smile on your face. How is this possible?

The book suggests fun strategies to help cut down your spending and repay your debt. Think of a 'no spend' day to raise the funds for clearing the smallest loan using your strategy. You simply look for alternatives that are fun, delicious, and highly reliable. When you complete the 'no spend' challenge, shed off an impulse spending behavior, and create a new line of revenue to reward yourself. It is part of the success journey.

- The core of this part is the development of a winning strategy to clear the debt your way. The 4-step debt eliminator helps simplify the process of clearing debt so that you can easily apply and start the journey to financial freedom. As the debt elimination strategy takes shape, this part will motivate you with reports of people who overcame debts and became financially free.

Your case is not unique. Others have cleared debts. You can also get out of debt.

Part Two: Building Wealth

This part was created to serve as a guide to help you start building wealth when you overcome the problem of debt. Unfortunately, many factors that had forced you to get into debts will still be there when you clear the debt or install systems of clearing it. This part serves four key things.

1. It helps you to become a better financial manager. This will go a long way in helping you stay on top of your finances. It recommends that you adopt financial automation and further assists you to create an emergency fund so that nothing will easily get you back to debt.
2. No matter the amount of income that you make every year, this book demonstrates that you can create additional revenue to help clear debt faster. Using the suggestions on this book, you will learn how to increase the streams of revenue and become the successful person you always wanted.
3. To ensure you stay on top of your financial operations, this part also demonstrates how to use your credit card to strengthen your credit score. This will be crucial to ensuring you do not miss important services by financial companies, telecom organizations, and government agencies because of a poor credit score.
4. As you start investing, this book takes a few steps ahead to help you understand the pitfalls that lay on the way. It helps you to understand pyramid schemes and how to avoid them. It also identifies specific areas of investment such as Mutual funds and Exchange Traded Funds (ETFs) that have helped people reach financial freedom faster than they expected.

Note that getting to financial freedom does not mean giving up all the fun things you cherish in your life. You do not need to forego meals out, make your own soap, or decline social invitations that just came your way. All that is needed is the right mindset and commitment. This is what this book is all about.

The two parts work together to help shape you into a new person. The strategies therein, the demonstrations, and highlighted investment opportunities, will help you to see life differently. The money you have is not little. Rather, it can help to grow your portfolio and make you a happier person.

By the time you are through reading this book, you will not be the same again. You will wish you had it about 10 years ago because it has all the ingredients for success.

Disclaimer: This book was written with the US citizen in the mind. Therefore, some companies, services, and apps might not be available in your jurisdiction.

Part 1: Paying off Debts

Chapter One: What Causes Debt

When you take a closer look at the current debt situation in the society, the main question that comes into the mind is: "What made it become this extensive?" The debt issue is a complex thing that has intensified so much in society to the point that people have started seeing it as a normal part of life.

From television advertisements to student forums, the main thing that appears in common to all is debt. People are getting into debts when they are still young but finding a way out appears a major problem. This first chapter explores the main reasons that make people get into debt and get stuck there.

How do People End up with Debt?

The route to debts often commences at a tender age as young people grow up seeing their parents and seniors struggle to pay loans and mortgages. The notion of debt starts becoming a normal thing. But this is not all!

Endless advertising on television channels and social media shouting *"low credit score is no problem, you can still get credit"* further strengthen the idea that every person has a debt. It creates an impression that you should also not worry about getting into debt because you are part of society. Debt is considered normal and acceptable.

The slippery path to debt becomes distinct when people decide to advance careers by attending college. Taking out a loan is likely to position your balance sheet in the wrong place because you are simply increasing debt at a point when no income is in sight to start repayment. By the time you clear college, you are expected to start repaying the loan. The chances are that your credit score will go down and reduce your chances of getting credit from financial institutions.

After getting employed, you will probably take a mortgage. Within a short while, the deductions to repay loans become overwhelming. Often, many people go for debt consolidation to help reduce high-interest debts. However, the cycle of debt begins again after the repayment burden eases. This results in further damage to your credit score and an inability to access financing.

In addition to the above cycle, there are also specific reasons that could easily get you into debt. Here are some of them:

- **Reduced income:** If your income goes down, the chances are that the expenses are likely to drive you into debt. This can happen if you lose a job or a disaster such as fire razes your business or workplace. When income shrinks, it is prudent to make an urgent effort to align your lifestyle with it. For example, if you used to go for expensive getaways every weekend, consider reducing them or do away with them until the income status improves.
- **Divorce:** Over 50% of the marriages in the United States end up in divorce. Such separation comes with a lot of financial constraints. Because the US law governs how money should be shared in the event of a divorce, the separating parties end up in debt as they seek the help of expensive attorneys to get a bigger chunk of family wealth.
- **Poor money management:** In many cases, poor budgeting results in debt. Many people who operate without a monthly budget find it difficult to track their expenses and easily engage in impulse spending.
- **Underemployment:** When people are underemployed, there is a tendency to feel the situation as a temporary one. Some people end up overspending hoping that a better paying job will help to fill the gap. However, overspending is likely to plunge you into debt if the underemployment situation persists.
- **Gambling:** This is one of the most entertaining pastimes for Americans today. However, it soon degenerates into a serious addiction that makes you simply want to place the next bet. Many people find the idea of winning millions irresistible even when they have been trying for years without winning anything.

The problem of betting is made worse by the easy availability of loans. Most betting companies do not mind whether you have poor credit score when providing loans. They encourage you to continue borrowing and keep following the big jackpots. Gambling is an effortless way of mortgaging your future.

- **Medical bills:** When people fall ill, it is very easy to slide into debt trying to clear associated bills. The problem is aggravated by the fact that many medical facilities have become impatient and are turning patients into credit reporting agencies, resulting in damage to their credit scores.
- **Little or no savings:** Because of the ever-rising cost of living, the bulk of people's income is being used for expenses such as food, mortgage, transport, and school fees for the kids. However, failing to make ample savings means that you are not prepared for the unexpected. Therefore, when an emergency strikes, the chances are that you will end up falling deeper into debt.
- **Ignorance:** A large proportion of people in debt today are in the situation because they lack info about annual percentage rate (APR) on their credit cards. They do not know the amount they are charged as interest on their credit cards or the implications that arise from minimum payments. For example, the expectation is that if a loan of $100 and is charged an APR of 10%, the cost would be $10 per year. But it is more than that when it comes to credit cards, mortgages, and car loans[2].

APR on your credit card is compounded to include fees and interest charges so that the amount you are required to pay per year is higher than you would anticipate. Though the loan with the lowest APR is no doubt a cheaper option, it is important to carefully decipher the calculations and, where possible, avoid lagging behind the repayment schedule.

- **Lack of Motivation and Guidance:** When people recite the route that took them to debts, one thing that comes out clearly is that the problem started early in life. Many young people, especially those outside of financial careers, are rarely given comprehensive training on financial freedom. For example, many financial concepts appear new especially to graduates in non-business areas of specialization.

Society has to take its own share of the blame. Both Federal and individual states should reconsider ingraining financial related training starting from an early point in people development. At a personal level, parents, communities, religious leaders, and other entities need to start talking about the debt and how to avoid it.

---

[2]The Balance, 2019, *How to Calculate Annual Percentage Rate (APR).* <available at >https://www.thebalance.com/annual-percentage-rate-apr-315533

- **Increase in Rental Income:** The cost of living has been growing steadily over the years but the income of most people has stagnated. For example, the cost of rental prices in most cities has increased in the last two decades forcing people to seek loans to make ends meet. For those who want to own homes, the cost of mortgages has also gone up. This implies that you are likely to take longer repaying your home mortgage which can affect your ability to meet the cost of other personal needs.
- **Not making debt a priority:** If you are in debt, failing to prioritize it in your financial planning can prolong your debt and make it worse. In some cases, people do not realize they are even in debt! However, when you appreciate the problem, dig for more info to learn about it, and make it a priority, it becomes possible to overcome it.

Important Facts about Debt that Need to Know

To comprehensively explore the topic of debt and how to overcome it, you need to appreciate the magnitude of the problem. It appears that from individuals to companies, the problem of debts keeps getting worse year after year. Here are some important facts that you need to know about debt.

1. **The United States citizens' debt is in excess of $12.58 trillion.** If you toal the debts that American citizens owe on their credit cards, student loans, mortgages, and car loans among other credits, the answer is more than $12.58 trillion[3]. This is indeed more than the Chinese GDP! Of this debt, about two-thirds is a mortgage.
2. **The Standard American Household has a debt of $16,091 on credit cards alone.** If you look at the national debt, the figures are frightening. However, the numbers do not give the entire truth of the actual problem. The average household in the United States has a debt burden of about $16,091 according to Nerdwallet[4].
3. **Car loan delinquencies have risen to 21%.** If you thought that credit card loans are the only serious problem, think again. Auto loans are also a serious debt problem for most Americans. According to the St. Louis Federal Reserve Bank, United States

[3] The Balance, 2019, *How to Calculate Annual Percentage Rate (APR).* <available at >https://www.thebalance.com/annual-percentage-rate-apr-315533

[4] ibid

residents have about $1 trillion in auto loans. Between 2012 and 2017, delinquencies on auto loans grew to 21%[5].

However, it is important to appreciate that defaulting an auto loan can be a major problem because your car can be repossessed. This could, in turn, make it difficult to go to work or run your enterprises.

4. **Student loans are in excess of $1 trillion.** When learners take student loans for higher education, the anticipation is that they will get employment and clear the debt a few years after clearing college. However, the plan rarely takes shape. Instead, many students find themselves wallowing in major debts years after graduating from college. According to the New York Federal Reserve Bank, the student loan debt in the US stands at $1.31 trillion and takes up 10% of the total American debt[6].

It is important to appreciate that defaulting on student loan could easily damage your credit score and put your social security income into jeopardy. Indeed, even those who are paying their student loans opt to shelf buying new homes and starting families.

5. **Generation X and Baby Boomers have the highest level of debt.** Though millennials could have the baggage of student loans, you will be surprised to realize that they are not the cohort with the largest debts in the United States. Instead, the Baby boomers and Generation X have the biggest chunk of American Debt. People in the above two groups have more than $42,000 in non-mortgage debts[7].
6. **Debt has a positive correlation with depression.** It is not uncommon for people to feel overwhelmed by piles of unpaid bills and loans that require processing every month. Now, this has been linked to negative impacts on mental health. In one of the studies done by the University of Wisconsin, short-term debts such as credit card loans are linked to the high prevalence of depression symptoms. However, the study established that long-term debts do not cause anxiety because many people see

---

[5] ibid

[6] Megan, E, 2017, *15 Scary Facts about Debt that Should Alarm you*. <available at> https://www.cheatsheet.com/money-career/facts-about-debt-may-alarm-you-today.html/

[7] Megan, E, 2017, *15 Scary Facts about Debt that Should Alarm you*. <available at> https://www.cheatsheet.com/money-career/facts-about-debt-may-alarm-you-today.html/

them as part of their investment[8].

7. **A lot of people underestimate their debts.** While sliding into debt that lasts for decades is really bad, you will be surprised to realize that most people underestimate their debts. If you sum up the total amount of credit card debts that people say they have and compare with the actual figures from credit card companies', a huge discrepancy of over $415 million is evident[9]. However, why the big discrepancy?

Many people rarely give the actual amount of debt they owe to avoid being embarrassed. However, denial about your credit status can escalate an already bad situation.

8. **With Commitment, it is Possible to Get out of Debt.** Though the problem of debt is distressful, it is possible to address it. When people appreciate that they are in debt and commit to overcoming the problem, it is possible to become debt free. Most successful people today were at some point entangled in financial debts.

The interesting thing about debt is that when you decide to tackle it, the lessons become very important in helping you grow financially. For example, lessons such as cutting unnecessary costs are used to help raise money even for other ventures such as personal investment.

[8] Digangi, C, 2015, *The Scary Link Between Credit Card Debt and Depression.* <available at> http://money.com/money/3848551/credit-card-debt-depression/

[9] Ibid

Chapter Two: Examples of Debt and Why You Should Care

When you fall into debt, it creates a chain of problems that could affect every part of your life. In many cases, people tend to underestimate the impact of debts until it is too late. This chapter explores the impact of debts and why you should appreciate it and start caring. Additionally, it also outlines examples of debts.

Main Problems that can Result from Debt

When you are in debt, it becomes like a strong chain that makes you stall in the same position for many years. Because of the debts, most financial institutions will look at you as a high-risk party and decline applications for credit. This implies that you will also find it difficult to fund personal development.

In a couple of years, your close friends will be having big companies and growing them to the next level as you stagnate in the same place. Well, you cannot afford to continue hiding when you have debts. It is time to address them head-on and become successful. Here are additional reasons why you should care.

- Health Deterioration

If you take too long before paying your debt, your name will be forwarded to collection agencies that will go after you. The agencies will call regularly demanding that you pay the debt. In some cases, this could easily become a legal battle. The stress that comes with such demands could end up causing problems such as migraines and poor health.

- Damage to Your Credit Score

When you fall into debt, your credit score will drop drastically. Because the credit score is a measure of your creditworthiness, a poor score implies that no financial institution will agree to lend you money. Note that it is not just the financial organizations that are using credit scores today. You are also likely to get an application for phone credit and a mortgage declined.

As most lines of credit get closed, you will be left with few financial options such as payday loans that are very expensive. But these loans only risk sinking you deeper into debt. Note that in the event that you default on the payday loan, the interest rates could become higher plunging you deeper into debt.

Regrets

When you look at your current debt situation, one of the main problems will be regrets. You will start wondering what actually made you get into the problem of debt. This will grow from personal regrets to blaming other people such as your parents, close friends, and community.

- Strained Relationships

If you have a lot of debts, the chances are that your relationship will get strained. Debts impact financial related stress and can result in emotional and mental issues. Depending on how the debt accumulated, it could result to trust issues and even divorce. About 80% of couples who get divorced in the US indicate financial problems to be one of the primary causes[10].

- Low Productivity at Work

As the impact of debt becomes evident, the psychological effects are likely to be felt even at the workplace. You will feel odd as other people talk about their success stories with money and new ventures. To fit in their circles, you will be forced to create lies. This could culminate to self-guilt and more regrets. Ultimately, your productivity at work will take a downturn.

The main reason why you should care is that though you are in debt, it is not a permanent problem. This means that you can still get out of it and reach your financial goals. But how do you do it?

You will only need to develop the right mindset and commit to clearing it. You will be surprised to know that a lot of people who are very successful today were at one point wallowing in debt. You can start by cutting off excesses in your lifestyle and directing the

---

[10] CreditLoan, 2019, How Debt Affects Relationships and What to Do About It. <available at> https://www.creditloan.com/blog/how-debt-affects-relationships/

cash to clearing debts. You should also consider creating new lines of revenue to further attack the debt. With a clear plan, your debt can be erased!

Examples of Debts

1. A student loan of $30,000, requiring minimum repayment of $50 per month (Federal Direct Student Loan, interest 4%)

Standard loan repayment plans are considered the default status of most credits unless the terms and conditions indicate otherwise.

With the standard loan repayment of a $30,000 loan being $50, you might want to consider paying more to clear it within the stipulated time frame.

When this loan is offered at an interest rate of 4% and a repayment period of 120 months, the monthly payment would come to $304. Then, the total interest paid in the course of the entire repayment session would be $6,448 culminating to a total of $36,448.

2. A student loan of $30,000, requiring minimum repayment of $50 per month (Federal Direct Student Loan, 6% monthly interest)

When this loan is offered at an interest rate of 6%, the monthly repayment would come to $333. The total interest paid for the loan in the course of a 10 year period would come to $9,967. This would push the total loan repaid to $39,967.

The main difference between the total amount repayable in the first loan and the second one is $3,519 for the same period of 10 years. This means payment of an additional $29/month. To pay the same total amount like the first loan, you would require paying a sum of $2,900 before the interest is applied.

3. A student loan of $30,000 (Income-based repayment, 4% interest rate, average monthly repayments on $47,000 per year)

It is important to note that income-based repayments (IBR) are only provided to graduates who qualify for them. The repayment takes a certain percentage of the learner's discretionary income to repay the credit. This means that the monthly income is dependent on how much you earn. If you are new, the rate is pegged at 10% but should not exceed ten years. Note that the median income for US college students is considered $47,000.

Therefore, if you take a $30,000 loan, the repayment will range from $245 and $304 every month. The total interest paid during a 10-year and 8-month period would be $7,141. This would bring the total payable amount to $37,141 by the time the entire loan is cleared.

Chapter Three: The Scary Psychology behind Impulse Spending

We have at one time or another fallen victim to impulse spending. Maybe you had simply taken a friend to the mall but ended up spending some money on a new dress. This happens because buying is an emotional process as opposed to a logical one.

This chapter is a closer evaluation of the psychology of impulse spending to demonstrate what it is and identify harmful spending patterns.

A Closer Look at the Psychology of Spending

Impulse buyers always look for items that will make them happy and elegant in front of others. This makes them easily fall prey to advertisements that promise ecstasy. However, the advertisements are designed as marketing strategies to capture the buyer's mind by shouting that the item on display is the best[11].

An impulse buyer may feel unhappy and believe that if they wear expensive clothes, then they will get happiness and respect from peers. This perception motivates the impulse buyer to set out shopping in the market. When they get into the mall, a well-displayed item will catch their attention and they will draw closer to check it out.

At that point, they might remember another friend who uses a similar item. Thoughts of buying the item and going with it create ecstasy. At this point, they cannot resist the urge to buy. They buy the item without assessing whether it is too expensive or even comparing it with alternatives.

At the end of it all, impulse buying results in remorse and brings unhappiness that the buyers wanted to avoid. However, the process cannot be reversed and they will have to incur additional expense looking for the right item[12].

---

[11] James, J, 2017, *Money, the Psychology of Money: Master Your Saving and Spending Habits.* New York: CreateSpace Independent Publishing Platform.

[12] Ibid

Factors that Fuel Impulse Spending

As shops invest more in marketing, buyers easily find themselves purchasing items they did not intend to buy. Here are some factors that influence impulse spending:

- **Fear of not finding the same item again**. Some people get overwhelmed when they enter a shop and get a customized item that no one else has. They end up buying it so they can look unique with an item that is not available elsewhere in the market.
- **Fear of missing out.** When a new product is launched, it is possible to see a lot of people getting interested. This could make you to also order the same product. A good example is when Apple releases a new iPhone and the orders are too many to keep up with.
- **Money availability.** When a consumer has a lot of funds that are easily accessible when shopping, the probability of impulse spending is very high. This is the primary reason why a lot of people overspend on their credit cards.
- **Discounts and offers.** When a product that you have always desired to own has a discount attached to it, you could be tempted to purchase it even if you had not planned to.
- **Love for shopping.** There are people who derive pleasure in simply entering a mall and picking items. Such people will even look for more expensive stores that match their status, even when items sold there are more costly.

Identifying Harmful Spending Habits

In this part, I will list ten non-essential things that I bought, the reason for buying them, and then note the harmful spending patterns.

1. **iPhone X.** I bought the phone because of the hype it attracted all over the globe. I wanted to enjoy the new features such as the dual camera, stronger processor and the bliss of having the latest model.
2. **Nike shoes.** I liked the display of the shoes and ended up buying because I had cash readily available in the credit card. I was impressed by the fact that the shoe shouted that I will be a champion when wearing them. However, this was a marketing strategy for Nike and the seller.

3. **A new Lenovo laptop.** I bought this new laptop because most of my colleagues in the workplace were using Lenovo. However, my HP Laptop was still in good condition.
4. **Antique furniture.** I was motivated to buy this piece of furniture from the fact that it was drawn from the 19th Century. It was a special collection and I wanted to feel unique for being the only one with such furniture.
5. **New television.** The main motivation was that it was a smart television that could easily help me get online. However, I rarely used the feature because I did most of the online tasks on the laptop and smartphone.
6. **Kitchen cutlery.** I was moved by the impressive display of the cutlery in the shop. Though I had purchased another set a few months earlier, I still ended up buying.
7. **New suit.** I went with my friend who was checking on his wedding suit, and I got carried away by the suit. It was interesting that the measurements perfectly suited me and I ended up buying with a credit card.
8. **A digital camera.** I like the idea holidaying in different parts of the world. When I found a Nikon camera with new specs, I was carried away. I imagined taking stunning early morning images on the great beaches of Hawaii or in Antarctica. I ended up buying the camera even though I still had another one that worked fine.
9. **Chandelier lamps.** While the lamps that I had at home were indeed great, the display and benefits that the marketer attached to the chandelier lamp made it irresistible. Indeed, I ended up spending more to have the lamps installed on the ceiling.
10. **Ice maker.** As a person who loves spending a lot of time outdoors, the idea of a great ice maker was very impressive. Though I had a smaller ice maker that served me well, I bought a new and bigger one because it was on discount.

After reviewing these non-essential items, I found a number of harmful spending patterns. First, my purchasing pattern was influenced by the attractive displays used in the store. This made me buy items without carefully reviewing whether they would deliver value to me.

I also established that having readily available cash also made me desire to buy new items on display. This was a harmful pattern because I ended up buying new items even if the current ones were still functional.

Friends were also influencing me to purchase new items even when I had not planned to. This was wrong because I got carried away and rarely checked the overall quality of the item being purchased.

My desire to outdo others drove me to look for opportunities that elevated me from them. This is the main reason that made me crave for items on sale which made me stand out. However, this does not mean that the items were always of higher quality. For example, the 19th Century furniture I bought ended up breaking in a few months. I had to revert to my previous corner sofa. It was a total waste of money.

When I realized the dangers associated with impulse spending, I had to redefine my shopping behavior. It was one of the strategies that helped me become financially free. You can also avoid impulse buying by following the tips outlined in the next part.

How to Avoid Impulsive Spending

While the deals on different items might look irresistible, you can avoid impulse spending by ensuring you always shop with a list. This will help you to only pick the items that you need and had planned to buy. Here are other tips to help you avoid impulse spending:

- **Adopt a waiting period rule.** This is a very important strategy because it gives you ample time to review an item to ascertain whether you need it and it is of high value. A good waiting period should be at least 24 hours.
- **Always calculate the value of the item before purchasing it.** Because impulse buying is mainly emotional, you can stop it by being logical. One way of doing this is thinking about the time you would require to earn what the item costs. For example, if a suit is tagged $200, you will need about ten hours if you're earning $20 per hour. Therefore, is it worth buying? This way, your mind will tell you to walk away.
- **Reevaluate what you own.** Impulse spending often results in a loss of money because people rarely think about what they own. If you evaluate your current iPhone 7 that has been fantastic, you will realize that it is still great and you do not need a newer iPhone X.
- **Set shopping procedures.** If you want to reach financial freedom faster, everything needs to follow a course. When it comes to shopping, it is important to

follow three steps before buying any item. First, determine you need the item, then review the quality of the item, and finally compare the price with others in the market.

- **Use a no-spend challenge.** No spend challenges are periods when you cut purchases and do with what you have. During such periods, the no spend rules indicate that you can only buy a few basics such as toiletries while the rest of the money goes to savings.
- **Avoid shopping inside the mall.** If you order your products online and pick them at the storefront, you will reduce the danger of buying items simply because they have been displayed well on the shelf.
- **Unsubscribe from retail newsletters.** Many stores use newsletters to push offers and discounts to targeted clients. These can tempt you to spend more than you had planned. It is advisable to unsubscribe from such notifications and follow individual stores only when looking for offers.
- **Do not shop before reading reviews.** If you can take a closer look at an item that is very attractive, it will be easy to make the right decision whether to purchase or not. You can do this by reading feedback from past users to know about their experience after using the item under consideration. Reviews from experts can also help you to compare it to other similar items on the market.
- **Think about the last unplanned purchase that you regret.** Impulse spending always results in regrets. If you purchased an item without planning last time and regretted the decision, use it to avoid similar experiences in the future. Make sure to ask this question before making a purchase: "Will you end up regretting it like last time?"
- **Leave behind people who like impulse spending.** If you are a family person, it is important to leave out the members who can make you buy more than you had planned. For example, consider leaving your child behind when shopping in a mall because they could pick items that you had not intended to buy.
- **Seek expert help.** If you find that impulse spending is becoming too difficult to stop, consider seeking expert assistance. Professionals can help you to see the problem and develop creative ways to avoid unwanted purchases.
- **Do not purchase items that cannot be returned.** In many cases, items that

have very low price tags are of poor quality and cannot be returned. This is very common with items on clearance sales. Therefore, if a product does not have a money back guarantee, simply walk away even if the price is tempting or the display makes it irresistible.

- **Avoid taking extra cash when going shopping.** When many people have extra cash in their pocket or credit card, the temptation to overspend is very high. Therefore, you can avoid overspending if the cash available is only enough to purchase the items you planned to buy.
- **Change your friends.** If you have friends who love shopping and seeking to influence others' buying habits, it might be time to walk away. As you target reducing impulse purchases, consider searching for friends who share the same dream. Such friends will always encourage you to take no-spend challenges and other saving tips.

Chapter Four: How to Pay off Debt in 4 Easy Steps

Being in debt is a major burden that can hold back your life from success. You will realize that it is even worse because most debts, such as credit card loans, keep attracting severe penalties. Therefore, you will need to craft a way of clearing the debt.

The good news to you is that paying off the debts is not as complicated as you might have previously thought. This chapter will provide you with a complete guide on how to clear the debt. It focuses on creating the right mindset, rewarding yourself, and avoiding complicated budgeting procedures. The chapter also explains the 4-step debt eliminator method, shows you how to save on bank fees, and ends with a guide for a no-spend Challenge.

Creating the Right Mindset to Clear Your Debt

Getting the right mindset to tackle your debts is perhaps the first step in any march to financial freedom. Though it can take some time because society appears to encourage people to borrow and buy more, it is definitely worth it. If you find that the debt is starting to get out of control, simply drag it into the light and face the reality. Here is how to create the right mindset.

- Acknowledge the Debt

Today, many people do not admit that they are in debt. In some cases, you might not even be aware of the debt value because you have loans from multiple credit cards, bank, student loan and mortgage among others. Therefore, you need to acknowledge the debt and initiate own interventions before creditors start knocking.

You can do this by grabbing a notebook or opening a spreadsheet to list all the debts. How much do you owe in student loans, credit cards, car loans, and departmental stores among others? This will be the first step to creating a debt management plan[13].

- Accept your Debt and Move On

[13] Ramsey, D, 2013, The Total Money Makeover: A Proven Plan for Financial Fitness. London: Thomas Nelson

It is human to blame yourself about the current situation. Make sure to deal with emotions such as anger, regret, and guilt as opposed to sweeping them under the carpet. You could even consider seeking some help about the problem so that you start dealing with it.

What is more important is that you need to forgive yourself and move on. What made you fall into debt will become part of the learning process so that you can avoid similar problems in the future. When you finally get out of debt, it will be a milestone. But you need to start somewhere.

- Get Motivation from Those Who Have Managed to Address Debts

When you are in debt, there is a tendency to think that your problem is unique. However, it is not. The reality is that many people have been in debt and managed to get out. These should be your source of motivation. For example, Richard managed to clear his $40,000 debt after developing the right mindset (Read more success stories of people who overcame debts later in this chapter).

- Come up with a Game Plan to Clear the Debt

After accepting that you are in debt and developing the desire to clear it, it is time to craft a game plan. This will be your strategy to steadily reduce the debt until it is eliminated completely. One of the components of your plan should be reducing spending in non-essential areas and directing the funds to clear the debt. You should also consider creating additional streams of revenue to help clear the debt faster.

- Reward Yourself when you Make every Milestone

To make the process of clearing debt fun, it is important to plan rewarding yourself. Do not see the process as a form of punishment. Just like a job promotion, you should reward every effort and milestone. For example, if you have a debt of $40,000, consider rewarding yourself with a token after clearing every $1,000, $5,000, and $10,000 respectively. This will help you to appreciate the current effort and offer additional motivation to keep moving on.

- Keep the Process as Simple as Possible

When you are trying to make things work or starting a long journey of repaying your debts, it is important to keep everything as simplified as possible. It is particularly important to avoid complicated budgeting procedures. Instead, you should consider using the standard budgeting spreadsheet to help you plan for the available revenue, what to pay for which loan, clear other expenses, track personal financial goals.

To track the entire process, consider setting reminders on your diary, computer, and phone. This will remind you when it is time to do the next budgeting, make some payment, or reward yourself after hitting a milestone.

The Four Step Debt Eliminator

No matter how big your debt appears, all that you need is a positive mind and a debt clearing strategy. This is why the 4-step debt eliminator strategy (commonly referred to as the debt snowball method) is recommended in most situations.

A Closer Look at the 4-Step Debt Eliminator Strategy

This debt eliminator method is aimed at motivating you to keep reducing the debt by attacking it, starting with the one that has the lowest amount. Once the smallest loan is knocked down, the amount that was used to repay it is directed to the subsequent small loan. The method works because of two things.

- You are able to pay a minimum amount required for all your loans. This implies that your credit cards, auto loans and other lines of credit will not add penalties that can increase the debt.
- By removing one debt after another, you can see some visible results. If you had initially thought that repaying debts is impossible, seeing a few of the loans drop off will provide a lot of motivation to clear the remaining amount[14].

How to use the 4-Step Debt Eliminator

This debt elimination method requires you to only follow four simple steps to achieve financial freedom[15]. Take a look

- **Step 1: List your debts from smallest to largest regardless of interest**

---

[14] Ramsey, D, 2013, The Total Money Makeover: A Proven Plan for Financial Fitness. London: Thomas Nelson

[15] Ibid

rate. Before deciding what to give more focus or what to anticipate, make sure to list all the debts. This should include their particulars such as the required minimum monthly repayment and time. The aim is to get all the balances in one place and compare with the available revenue before starting the repayment process.

- **Step 2: Make minimum payments on all your debts except the smallest.** By paying the minimum amount for all the loans except the smallest one, you will not get delinquent.
- **Step 3: Pay as much as possible on your smallest debt.** When you direct the remaining resources to attack the lowest debt, it implies that it will be cleared faster.
- **Step 4: Repeat until each debt is paid in full.** Now that the smallest debt is cleared, you will need to direct the effort to the next small loan until it is also cleared. In a few months or years, it will come as a surprise to realize that only one or a few loans will be remaining. You will also be highly motivated to clear them faster.
- Sub-step – When you have multiple credit card loans, here are the main steps to follow.
    1. Make the minimum payment on all of your accounts
    2. Put as much extra money as possible toward the account with the highest interest rate
    3. Once that debt is paid off, start paying as much as you can on the account with the next highest interest rate. Repeat the cycle until all the credit card debts are paid

To demonstrate how the 4-step debt eliminator works, here is an example of John's debt.

- **Car Loan**: $20,000 at 6% with a monthly minimum repayment of $400.
- **Medical Loan**: $10,000 at 6.8% with a monthly minimum payment of $115;
- **Student Loan**: $5,000 at 6.8% with a monthly minimum payment of $60.

The required total minimum monthly repayment for John is $575. To clear the debt using the 4-step debt eliminator, John should plan to pay the minimum repayment amount for only the Car Loan and Medical Loan. This amounts to $515. Then, the rest of the finances should be directed at clearing the student loan.

Instead of only meeting the minimum repayment requirement for the Student Loan, John will attack it with more finances from his salary and other sources. For example, if he manages to pay $1000 for the student loan every month, it will take only five months to clear the smallest debt.

Once the Student Loan is cleared, the process should be repeated with the focus on the Medical Loan. This implies that the amount that John was using to clear the Student Loan should be directed at clearing the Medical Loan ($9,425 by the fifth month).

This process should be repeated until all the loans are cleared.

Useful Tips to Help Your Succeed when Using the Debt Eliminator

Though the debt eliminator method is easy to use, some people find it hard sticking to it and sometimes walk away when it is halfway. Here are some useful tips to use:

- **Look at the debt broadly, factoring all your sources of income.** As you list all the debts, it is also crucial to include all your sources of income. This will help you to understand the correct personal financial status and plan appropriately. For example, if you have a salary and a business that provides additional income, direct most of the resources towards clearing the debt.
- **Avoid falling back into debt.** In some cases, people have found themselves falling back into debt when the repayment burden eases. However, this could compromise the process you have taken a lot of time and resources to plan for. Instead of seeking debt, it is advisable to cut spending on non-essential items such as holidays and entertainment.
- **Plan for basic needs when using the debt eliminator.** One thing that you need to appreciate when trying to clear debt is that the basic needs have to be budgeted appropriately. For example, you should first deduct the money for rent, food, transport, kid's school fees, etc. before paying the loan.
- **Look for additional sources of income to clear the debt.** The primary target of using the debt eliminator method is to clear all the debts. Therefore, if you can make some additional income and direct it to knock off the debt, it will be cleared faster. Some great options include writing a book for sale on Amazon and blogging on your favorite topics.
- **Make sure to save for an emergency.** Even when making a lot of effort to clear the debt, an emergency can easily compromise everything. If your spouse falls ill and

requires specialized medical attention, it is very easy to direct your funds there. To avoid such a scenario, it is important to have an emergency fund. As you plan for basic needs, some funds should also go to the emergency fund. It is also important to take medical insurance for the entire family.

How to Save on Bank Fees

One method you can use to save money using banks, is selecting the one with low-interest charges. If you take the monthly bank statement, you will be able to see how much fees were charged on the account. To cut this fee, here are some steps that you can use:

- Compare different banks' fees and switch to the one with lower charges
- Compare accounts and select the one with lower fees
- Avoid using another bank ATM to withdraw your money because it attracts additional charges
- Where possible, consider using digital channels because most of them are free or have very small charges
- Request bank statements by email as opposed to physical deliveries to avoid delivery-related fees
- Ensure you understand the monthly caps for your accounts and ATM withdrawals to avoid additional charges

12 Ways to Save on Groceries

1. Stick to your Numbers when Shopping

Work on your grocery budget and stick to it. As you shop, have your calculator to ensure you stick to the budget. Here, the target is ensuring you understand the big picture of the financial debt to be cleared and attacking it bit-by-bit.

Remember that this will require you to shed off unnecessary content of your grocery list. For example, you can slash fast food from the list and stick to homemade, dried and crunchy fruits.

"We are under $80 a week for our family (two adults and a preschool kid). We have done away with pizzas. You can also do it and make a significant saving to help cut your debt."

2. Check your Store First

Before you set off buying new groceries, it is important to check the pantry for an alternative. That is right! Simply because you are out of one item does not imply you must head to the market. The chances are that you have an alternative that can be used.

If you like having a pineapple cocktail every evening, you can opt to do with the mangoes or apples because they are the options available in the fridge. Other substitutes you can use include preparing popcorns instead of rushing to the market for new cashew nuts.

"The idea behind using substitutes is that alternative food sources such as nuts, fruits, veggies, and meat provide the body with more minerals and nutrients. I'm on the second week and have managed to knock $231 by using substitutes."

3. It is Time to Start Storing your Meals

Preparing a meal costs so much! But you can cut this cost by a huge margin by preparing large meals and freezing the leftovers. Nothing beats already having it in the freezer.

Think of the effort, materials, and costs that go into preparing a meal. By preparing a big meal, you can save on energy and food materials such as spices that would have been used to prepare several meals.

"At first I found it hard to notice the impact. However, I established that my food reserves were going for longer as the power bill shot down. After comparing last month and others, I managed to save $209."

4. Round up your Grocery Estimates

Keeping track of your grocery expenses helps to ensure you are on top of the budget all the time. However, there are times when the cost of items does not match with your estimates. For example, the price of an item on your budget list could be $5.26. To avoid getting surprises, it is advisable to round up the cost to full figures.

"Rounding the price to complete figures such as $5.26 to $6.0 means that your budget will always cover the listed items. I regularly check the price of different items on the list especially when budgeting to ensure I make the estimates as precise as possible."

5. Utilize the Scan it Feature

After budgeting, the main question remains; “How do you operate within the boundaries of the defined limit?” Most grocery stores today have a ‘Scan It’ feature that allows you to walk around and scan items on sale as you shop.

Scanning the items helps you follow the totals to avoid getting surprised. The Scan It feature also helps you to decide whether some items that you had selected are really necessary.

“I like the Scan It feature because it helps me to check alternatives that I can pick at the same or lower price. Instead of queen cakes, the Scan It feature helps me to pick alternatives such as donuts.”

6. Work and Stick to Your Meal Plan

When planning for meals, factor the offers from a specific store. For example, a store that has opened new offers on an item of interest is a great place to get your purchases. Then, buy in large quantities and freeze the supplies. Try to avoid shopping when hungry because you are likely to impulse buy the items on the shelf.

“By planning meals well, I am able to evaluate the nutrient needs and even negotiate for lower rates. On average I am able to save about 10% by sticking to the meal plan and pitching a tent on stores releasing new discounts.”

7. Only Buy what you Need

Many are the times when you will get tempted to buy an item because it is discounted. Though that item is marked one for $5 and four for $10, it does not mean that you have to buy it. The chances are that you will end with a surplus going into waste.

“I always work with what I need. First I draw a plan of what to buy and only pick such offers when they fall within the budgetary limits. For example, if I had planned to buy an item for $5 but the store has an offer of two for $5, it is okay.”

8. Shop Online as Opposed to Visiting the Mall

When you walk into a mall, the temptation to pick more items from the shelves is at times irresistible. But there is a way out. You can purchase the items of interest online instead of visiting the mall.

"After realizing this secret and its potential to help build savings, I advised my wife to always prepare a list of all the items we need. Then, we order them online and drive to the store to pick them up. This way, we are able to save time and avoid walking into the store. It is also convenient for us because we have little kids."

9. Plan to Eat Dinner Leftovers for Lunch

The common practice in many homes is preparing a nice dinner and taking lunch in a restaurant or hotel. For others, both dinner and lunch are bought from cafes. This can raise your overall cost of food with a great margin. Here is a way out.

Instead of going to a café, consider preparing a great dinner every night and using the leftovers for lunch. This means that you can enjoy more nutritious foods and save the money that could have gone to buy the food.

"Because my husband and I work near our living house, lunches for Monday to Thursday are taken from supper leftovers. We have saved more than $1200 since we started the plan."

10. Buy Generic

If you take a closer look at the leading sellers in the market today, their products have a very high price tag. In most of the cases, these stores want to attract a specific type of clientele. However, most of the food they sell is junk and unhealthy.

"To make some savings, we shop at the grocery stores that have made a name for low price products and focus on buying generic stuff. We have cut junk such as pizzas from our budget that helps save about $250 while generic stuff further cuts about $250 per month.

11. Only Buy Meat when on Sale

Meat can be expensive depending on the preferred choice. For example, boneless skinless chicken thighs are cheaper compared to chicken breasts. To keep the cost of proteins low, you could also consider alternatives such as legumes that are also delicious.

"At home, my wife and I are always on the lookout for the stores have an offer on meat. The good thing is that the offers are announced every few days by different stores. Besides, we have also subscribed to the stores for notifications when such offers are announced. This way, we are able to save between $250 and $350 every month."

12. Do Not go Shopping with Over-spenders

If you want to save on groceries, the over-spenders should always be left behind. In many cases, they insist that you add more items even though it was not included in the list. For example, the attractive display of oranges and pineapples can easily make over-spenders add them to the shopping cart though the target item was passion fruits.

"In my family, the over-spender is my husband. He can end up filling the shopping cart even when the aim was picking only a packet of milk. By leaving him behind when am going to the grocery store helps me save an average of $400 per month."

Debt Success Stories

No matter your debt situation, the reality is that you can overcome it. Here are some debt success stories you should read:

1. Richard, a Biologist Cleared $40,000 Debt

When speaking to frugality magazine called *The Disease Called Debt*, Richard revealed that his debt problem started with the higher education loan. Then, he slid further into $40,000 debt after taking an auto loan and a series of credit card loans[16].

Richard's ability to overcome the debt was made possible by his commitment. He indicates that he tried with a number of methods until he got the one that worked in his situation.

Living without debt for Richard helps him to enjoy life and become more productive. He indicates that when he was in debt, his hands and indeed life were tied so that it was impossible to reach full potential. Now, he can afford a vacation and enjoy good times with family without worrying about a nagging debt problem.

Richard explains that his health has also improved. Unlike during the time when he was in debt, he can now afford to relax, do more exercises, and spend more time with the family. All of these have reduced problems such as migraines that were initially common to him.

---

[16] Disease called Debt, 2018, *Debt Success Stories: Richard Paid off $40,000 in Debt.* <Available at>https://diseasecalleddebt.com/debt-success-stories-richard/

Richard emphasizes that the biggest thing that bogged him down when he was in debt were thoughts about how to overcome it. However, he advises people to appreciate the problem and take it head-on.

2. Heron Abegaze and Elijah Bankole Paid Thousands of Debt in Just Three Years

Attacking debt and knocking it down is possible if you evaluate your life and target the areas where you can slash spending. This is the trick that Abegaze and Bankole used to clear off nearly $162,000 of debt. The couple attacked the debt with savings raised by declining friends' invitations, postponing holiday, and foregoing fancy cars[17].

For the couple, there is nothing as enjoyable as relaxing on a weekend with a spouse without worrying about the debt burden. It makes life foggy and could even wreck a relationship. Today, Abegaze and Bankole recite their journey with enthusiasm about the strength of their bonds.

The couple has also learned about the importance of transparency and communication in a relationship. As a couple, knowing about the status of the debt and love for each other made them combine synergies and clear it together. If Bankole was alone, the journey could probably have taken longer.

However, the most important thing that Bankole insists about the entire journey is the lessons they have learned. They have come to appreciate that there is nothing that one cannot do with correct planning. The tricks used to save the money have helped the couple to also become successful in their investments.

3. Melanie Lockert Cleared her $81,000 Student Loan

Back in 2013, Lockert had a student loan of about $81,000. But the scary thing about it was that she was unable to find steady work that could help her to pay the loan faster. Therefore, she ventured into the pool of self-employment and started blogging to try and get money for sustenance and repaying the loan[18].

---

[17] Judith,O, 2018, *How this Couple Paid Off Nearly $162,000 Of Debt In 3 Years.* <Available at > https://www.refinery29.com/en-us/2018/03/194339/how-one-couple-paid-off-all-their-debt

[18] Adam, H, *21+ Motivational Stories About Getting out of Debt.* <available at> https://adamhagerman.com/21-get-out-of-debt-stories/

The effort paid off when her income tripled what she was earning when employed. To clear the debt, she set a target and budgeted well to prioritize the student loan. She managed to clear her debt earlier than one year.

Since breaking away from debt, Lockert has shifted to her dream city, Los Angeles, where she still runs her blog. She indicates that the freedom she has earned has helped her change perspective in life. Unlike in the past, there is nothing that she cannot achieve with proper planning and budgeting.

For Lockert, the idea of being able to fully control finances has ushered in a new beginning. She sees the debt era as a crucial learning phase that simply prepared her for bigger roles in the society. This is why she says that her life and success are only getting started and the world of opportunities is fully open for her. It is a new dawn.

4. Jackie Beck and Her Husband Paid Over $152,000

Beck and her husband found themselves with a debt problem of $152,000 that included a mortgage. However, about $52,000 was consumer debt that largely came from their credit cards. To clear the debt, Beck and her husband planned to attack it by first creating an emergency fund[19].

By attacking the debt together, it was possible to clear it faster and start enjoying financial freedom. But the couple indicates that this revealed their hidden potential to achieve greater things. They have started exploring new areas of investment and target being equally successful by applying the same strategies.

As a couple, clearing the debt together has helped them understand the love they have for each other. The debt was seen as the dark moments in their lives. By sticking together, they now believe that nothing can come between them no matter how complicated it is.

Waking up every morning and taking your breakfast without worrying that a recovery agency is on your back or a bank will come knocking is a great achievement for Beck. She indicates that they have found new happiness because it is now possible to take more time together, love more, and grow together.

---

[19] Adam, H, *21+ Motivational Stories About Getting out of Debt.* <available at> https://adamhagerman.com/21-get-out-of-debt-stories/

Beck says that she has also learned the tricks of falling into success; planning for everything. She indicates that her family no longer spends what it does not have because it is the roadmap to debts.

5. Deacon Hayes Paid off $52,000 in 18 Months

For Deacon and his wife, being in debt was a major cause of family strain. However, he believed that it was possible to clear it and live a happy life. He started by selling off unnecessary stuff including his car to clear the loan. Now, he is working on clearing the mortgage in ten years.

As a couple, Hayes points out that being bound by chains of debt is dangerous. Most of the debts, especially those based on credit cards, keep growing and you might end up dying in debt. But Hayes discovered the secret of commitment and persistence in clearing debts[20].

Today, Hayes explains that he has found new freedom because he can enjoy every moment of their lives without someone calling to bother them about debts. They no longer fear that they can be denied more credit to advance their business because of poor credit score. It is truly a free world!

When Hayes talks about the journey to financial freedom, he always insists on the importance of having support from loved ones. As he sold off his car and started a frugal lifestyle, he had the support and love from his wife. Taking the journey together makes it easy even when the going gets tough.

[20]Adam, H, *21+ Motivational Stories About Getting out of Debt.* <available at> https://adamhagerman.com/21-get-out-of-debt-stories/

Chapter Five: How to Do a "No Spend Challenge"

If you want to save more money to pay debts or build your portfolio, a No Spend Challenge might be the right option for you. At first, many people ask; "How can one stay without spending?" Well, if you are surprised, I had initially also thought it was an uphill task until I tried it.

A No Spend Challenge is a great method to jump-start big savings goals or even knock off the last part of a nagging debt. More importantly, when you stop spending over a period of time, it is a learning session to help you break shopping addiction, avoid living from paycheck to paycheck, and opening your world of opportunities. You will learn that nothing in life is impossible through planning and commitment.

This chapter is a comprehensive guide on how to do a No Spend challenge. It helps you to pick the right time-frame, select the allowances, and finally outlines useful tips to help you succeed in the challenge.

How to Do a No Spend Challenge

The first thing you need to do is deciding the type of No Spend challenge that you want to do. Here, you will need to set two important components; Allowances and Time Frame.

1. Select the Allowances

Allowances in a No Spend challenge is the amount that you are allowed to spend. At this point, you might need to go back and define the difference between a *want* and *need*. For example, if you take the case of a *need* such as food, you might want to narrow down to groceries only or *groceries* and some *restaurants* on special occasions[21].

Other examples of needs that should be included in the allowance include medical products, toiletries, and gas. Note that when you list an item such as toiletries, it is important to be specific. For example, you are allowed to spend on toilet paper.

---

[21] Ramsey, D, 2013, The Total Money Makeover: A Proven Plan for Financial Fitness. London: Thomas Nelson

The primary target is ensuring you create a complete list of needs for reference during the challenge. This will help you to know what you are allowed to spend on and what is forbidden.

2. Select the No Spend Time-frame

There are many no spend time-frames you can select. However, you are encouraged to start from the shorter time-frames and work your way up. Here are the main time-frames to consider:

- ***No Spend Day Challenge***

The No Spend day challenge is an ideal point for starters who want to test how much they can save before making a decision to advance to longer time-frames. Because it only focuses on a single day, the focus is limited to only a few activities. However, they could have a great impact on helping clear debts or build savings.

1. Look for free entertainment events instead of paying for them
2. Consider cooking at home as opposed to eating in a restaurant
3. Walk or cycle around instead of using the family car
4. Take time to explain the challenge to the family members and bond together. Their support will be very important especially when you start taking longer No Spend time frames.

Before you can move on to the next challenge, it is advisable to repeat the No Spend day challenge for a number of times. Remember to carefully review how much you saved during the challenge as a motivation.

- ***No Spend Week Challenge***

When you decide to take this challenge, it is important to have a clear list of things you do on the specified week. Here are some of the main activities that you should consider for the No Spend week challenge.

1. Consider preparing weekly meals and using them without going to a restaurant. However, if your allowance allows you to spend in a restaurant, consider limiting the amount to spend there
2. Make sure to prepare coffee or tea at the workplace instead of rushing to the

restaurant during the breaks. If your workplace does not allow you to prepare beverages, carry some from home

3. Instead of paying for a fitness club, consider walking or engaging in activities that bring together family and friends. For example, you can plan to walk with friends or cycle in the evening with other family members
4. Because you have a whole week to cut spending, it is time to do some chores that would otherwise require hiring someone. Good examples include washing your car and cleaning the carpet
5. Consider reading free books on the open library, Library of Congress, and internet archives as opposed to paid libraries.
6. It is also important to get involved in family fun activities such as painting that can help you achieve the main goal of not spending in the week

The same way you reviewed the No Spend day challenge, it is important to repeat for the weekly challenge. This will demonstrate the progress you are making and help motivate you to try longer No Spend periods.

- ***No Spend Month Challenge***

When you repeat the No Spend week challenges, a habit of spending on what is important and leaving non-important components out will start developing. As you start the No Spend month challenge, you will be asking the question: "Is this item really necessary?"

You will learn to get satisfied with the items you have and focusing on getting the best from them. Here are some key activities to consider during the No Spend month challenge:

1. Consider taking more time with the family as opposed to leaving for holiday. This will help you cut the cost of the flight, camping, and all the foods you would have eaten during the holiday. Instead, you can have great times with the family in the backyard.
2. Prepare do-it-yourself gifts for the family instead of buying them from the store. This activity will make the family more engaged and strengthen your bonds.
3. Plan to do common repairs on the house instead of calling a technician. The good thing is that you can easily follow video guides on repairing house parts such as roofing or wall painting.

4. During the week, consider using public transport or riding to work. This will help to promote your physical fitness as you continue saving money.
5. On entertainment, consider subscribing to free video channels as opposed to visiting the theaters. This will also help you to take more time with the family.

What to Do after a No Spend Challenge

It is important to appreciate that No Spend challenges can be difficult especially if are getting started. When you go through a challenge, it is prudent to pat yourself on the back. You have made it! But before reverting to the older ways, it is important to also do the following:

1. Establish how much money you have saved during the challenge. It is important to be specific and ensure that the funds are directed to a specific course. For example, you can use the funds to reduce debts, build savings, or enlarge the emergency funds.
2. What did you learn during the No Spend period? Though the primary goal of the challenge was to save money, there will be a lot to learn along the way. For example, you will learn that involving your spouse and the entire family to tackle a challenge makes the process easy.
3. Establish the obstacles that you want to conquer during the next challenge. Though you were determined to stick to the No Spend plan, some challenges such as festivities might have made it difficult to complete the entire challenge. Draw measures to address these difficulties.
4. Establish when the next challenge should be. Though you thought that raising $1000 to repay a debt is hard, the No Spend challenge has helped you to raise more! Such motivation will make you look forward to the next challenge. Remember that if the weekly challenge was a success, it is advisable to go for a monthly challenge. Indeed, you could even extend it to a few months.

Sit down with a pen and paper to look at the bigger picture of the No Spend idea. For example, if you take a $30 lunch every day, think of the amount that will be saved if you save that for 100 days (about three months). It will be $30*100=$3000. This is the motivation you need to keep moving on with the challenges.

Tips for Successful No Spend Challenge execution

While the calculations of how much you will save during the challenge can be impressive, it is important to appreciate that some people end up failing midway. These are useful tips to help make your No Spend challenge successful.

1. Start By Determining Why You Want To Undertake the Challenge

To successfully complete a No Spend challenge, it is important to establish why you are doing it. This becomes the driving factor to help you overcome the urge to rush to the theaters or do away with a holiday for a simple home movie. The goal could be building your savings or reducing your debt.

2. Set the Rules of The No Spend Challenge

Creating some rules will act like a boundary that tells you do not go beyond a specific point. The rules include things such as the allowances, the time-frame, what not to eat and places to avoid. To ensure that the rules are implemented, it is important to put them at a point where they are easily accessible. For example, display them on your living room wall, desktop, and even phone.

3. Discuss the Challenge with Family and Friends

It is important to point out that if you lack support from those close to you, the chances are that the challenge will not be successful. The family is especially crucial to helping you avoid excesses and optimize savings during the No Spend period.

If you have a spouse, they can help you especially in identifying alternatives as opposed to rushing to the grocery store when an item is out. Because your friends and family members want you to succeed, they will stick around to ensure you do.

4. Get Creative with what you have

If you take a closer look at your home, there are many ways of cutting cost by simply getting creative. For example, the beans in the store can be a great source of proteins instead of buying meat every other day. You can also prepare gift cards and use them for a family event as opposed to buying new things.

5. Remove Distractions that Encourage Shopping

As you start the No Spend challenge, it is important to appreciate that temptations to shop will still come your way. Therefore, you should avoid anything that encourages shopping. For example, you should unsubscribe to emails that regularly shout new deals on offer by a local store.

The time you take shopping should also be replaced with alternative tasks. For example, instead of going shopping on a Sunday afternoon, consider spending time with your family and playing games such as chess or watching movies. It can also be a great time to read a book or learn new skills.

6. Hide Credit Cards

When you go to buy an item during the No Spend period, having a credit card can encourage impulse buying. However, keeping the credit card away and only taking enough cash for specific items helps you to remain on course to optimize savings.

7. Engage in a Money Making Activity

Even as you put a lot of focus on cutting cost, it is advisable to also consider creating new streams of revenue. This will go a long way in helping to increase savings. Some good money making ventures include blogging, writing content for websites, selling photography, or part-time work in your area of specialization.

In some cases, people have started part-time money making ventures only for it to become their full-time work. For example, if you are an expert in a specific area such as health, vehicle mechanics, or agriculture, you could consider running a related blog.

8. Look for Motivation from People who have done No Spend challenges

Even if you are motivated by the primary goal of optimizing savings, it is also advisable to look at other people who have been successful. This will motivate you to also become successful. You can learn more tips for No Spend challenges and even new financial management skills.

Part Two: Building Wealth

Chapter Six: How to Automate Your Finances

If you take a closer look at your finances, the number of things that you are required to do can be overwhelming. You are required to prepare monthly budgets, remit money to repay loans, prepare financial accounts and many others. Is it possible to articulately manage all the tasks? The answer is "yes" when you use the right automation.

This chapter is a closer look at automation to help you manage your finances more prudently. It demonstrates why you need an emergency fund and further explores the leading financial app automation app, Mint.

Why you need an Emergency Fund

According to Murphy's law, "anything that can go wrong will go wrong". This means that even if you have taken the right measures to prevent accidents or bad occurrences, it is impossible to be 100% secure[22].

A company can go under. Employees can get laid off. Freelance work can be hard to get at some period. You can get sick. Bad things happen! Therefore, how do you deal with such situations? You need an emergency fund to help see you through the difficult period.

The need for an emergency fund is more important in today's professional climate than any other time in the past because the old model where people used to start working at 20 years of age and exiting at 55 years is no longer applicable[23]. Some people secure employment when they are well beyond 30 while others have only known contractual jobs.

---

[22] Chatterjee, A, 2016, Is the statement of Murphy's Law valid? *Complexity*, 21 (6): 374–380.

[23] IbID

How to Build an Emergency Fund

One thing that you need to know is that building an emergency fund cannot be done overnight. It requires commitment and a proper strategy. Here is an account of how to create an emergency fund.

1. **Set the long term emergency fund goal:** If you do not have a clear goal, it will be difficult to know where you are headed. You should create an emergency savings account, and then set meaningful and achievable goals[24]. The best thing is to budget for the emergency fund as you do for the loan and other needs.
2. **Build one month worth of savings in the emergency fund:** Look at the emergency fund through the lens of "What would happen if I lose my job today?" or "What would I do if a major financial emergency hits my family?" After saving funds worth one month of living, you have to move to the next level of growing it.
3. **Divide the additional cash you generate between savings and debt:** Whether you generate additional cash from a No Spend month or a new stream of revenue, make sure to divide the funds between the debt and emergency funds. If you are using the Snowball's 4-step debt eliminator, consider increasing the amount of funds going into emergency funds after knocking down the smallest loans.
4. **Take advantage of your employer's emergency funding:** If your employer provides an emergency cover, it means that you have a right to it. This means that you will not need to use your own emergency fund in case of a medical emergency because it is already covered.
5. **Avoid drawing funds from your emergency cover unless it is necessary:** As the name suggests, the emergency funds should only be used when unexpected events happen. Therefore, it should not be easy to reach the cash for regular shopping or even going on a holiday. If you want to raise money for holiday, consider saving it or tapping what is coming from passive income lines.

Apps you can use for financial automation

[24] Ramsey, D, 2013, The Total Money Makeover: A Proven Plan for Financial Fitness. London: Thomas Nelson

Financial automation has become the ultimate method to help people complete financial tasks, know the areas to slash spending, pay debts, and grow faster to financial freedom. One app that has stood out in the market because of its efficiency in financial automation is Mint. Here is a closer look at the app.

Mint

Mint is one of the leading finance automation applications designed to help you control all finances in one place. It is a free online service with over 15 million users across the globe. It only takes a few seconds to sign up and allows you to add multiple financial accounts to follow.

When you complete setting up the app, it downloads your financial data. It also downloads it every moment you visit[25].

The Mint dashboard allows you to do things like budgeting, set financial goals, and pools all the financial accounts in one place.

The Main Features of Mint

- **Budgeting and Tracking Expenses:** This is the primary feature of the application. It allows you to budget finances and further tracks the expenses to help you achieve personal financial goals.

To use the app for budgeting, simply navigate to the auto-categorization section to access the predefined categories for keying in budget items. It also allows you to create your own categories if the available templates are not impressive.

- **Creating and Managing Goals:** This feature is used to set and track goals. For example, you can set goals such as paying your debt or saving for a new home. The goals will be reflected in your monthly budget.
- **Monitoring Own Credit Score:** This feature allows you to track the entire financial picture and present them by simply clicking the "Show Details" button. The

[25] Jim, W, 2019, *Best Personal Finance Software apps of 2019.* <available at> https://wallethacks.com/best-personal-finance-software-apps/

feature shows important components of your credit rating such as the credit score, the age of credit accounts, payment history.

- **Prompt alerts:** When you get mint, it sends prompt notifications so that you can take timely actions. The app will notify you if you go over budget in a specific category, fall late with fees, or plan large purchases. It also reminds you when to pay bills.

One thing that makes Mint stand out from others is that it integrates with your mobile phone to ensure that you will never miss an alert or warning even when away. Besides, it also sends weekly reviews that you can use to carry further personal financial analysis with more advanced software or a financial expert.Why try to remember everything when automation software can help? Consider trying Mint.

Chapter Seven: Investing for Absolute Beginners

If you want to become successful, you have to invest. Investment provides you with an opportunity to grow and become the millionaire you have always imagined. However, investing can be scary because of the risks along the way. But you should not be scared because there is nothing that is risk-free.

This chapter provides beginners with useful insights on how to invest. It demonstrates how most successful people succeed in their investments and digs deeper into three main investment options; 401k (plus company match), Roth IRA, and Mutual Funds. Finally, it demonstrates why investment in housing returns 0% after inflation.

How Regular Folks Become Millionaires

Every time that the list of top billionaires in the globe hits the headlines, you are left with one question on the mind: "How did they make it?" However, a closer look at where most of them started reveals that they were ordinary folks who dared to dream and created a pathway to success. You too can become the next millionaire by following the strategies that they followed.

1. **Develop the right mindset:** Investment is all about the mindset. When you decide to invest and become successful, all the energies are directed there so that nothing will stand in the way. Do not let the risks that lay on the way misguide you. Make a decision and follow it to become successful.
2. **Learn from those who are already successful:** To curve your way to becoming successful in life, it is important to look at those who are already successful. This way, you can learn the methods they used and note the mistakes they made so that you can avoid them. Interestingly, you will find that some top minds such as Google and Apple founders started in a garage or in very difficult situations. Well, you can also make it.
3. **You do not have to start big to become a successful investor:** One misconception that some people hold is that you require a lot of money to start investing. The little you have is enough to start investing. If the investment portfolio of interest requires more, you can generate it by doing away with the non-essential

things at home. For example, you could sell a high-end car, buy a smaller vehicle for the family, and commit the extra funds to invest.

4. **Explore the best investment opportunities:** If you can identify good investment opportunities, rest assured that you'll enjoy impressive returns. Here, you should think of ventures that pay high returns such as mutual funds. Before you can venture into the selected investment option, make sure to carry comprehensive research about its operations and to develop the right expectations.
5. **Focus on creating multiple streams of revenue:** After commencing your investment, you have to keep working on new ventures. This will finally create multiple streams of revenue and catapult you into financial freedom.

When it comes to investing, there is no obstacle standing between you and success. Now is your time. Get out and grab that opportunity to become a millionaire!

Introduction to Compound Interest

Compound interest rate is a very useful tool when it comes to investment and saving. Whether you are saving money in a long term investment plan or an emergency fund, the accumulation of compound interest helps to boost returns.

Compound interest is the interest that is calculated on both the saved principle and accruing interest. It is calculated by multiplying the initial principle by one plus annual interest raised to the number of compound periods minus one (see the formula below)[26].

$A = P(1 + r/n)^{(nt)}$.

A = the future value of the investment/loan (it includes interest)
P = the principal investment amount or the initial deposit/ loan

r = the annual interest rate (decimal)
n = the number of times that interest is compounded annually
t = the number of years the money is borrowed or invested for

[26] Previte, J, and Hoffman, R, 2014, *Essential Financial Mathematics.* Washington: Lulu.com

NOTE: The above formula provides the actual value of an investment in the future, which is inclusive of compound interest + principle. Therefore, if you wish to narrow down to only compound interest rate, use the formula below[27].

Total compounded interest = $P (1 + r/n)^{(nt)} - P$

Compound Interest Impact on Investment

When your investment return is based on compound interest, your portfolio will grow rapidly because the interest is calculated on both the principle and the accrued interest. For example, if you put $100 into a saving scheme that has compounded interest rate of 10%, it will be worth $110 by the end of the first year. However, if it stays there for another year, the new principle will be $110. Therefore, the p by the close of the second year will be $21 and the total principle $121.

Take another example of a person who joins a mutual fund offering 7% compounded interest rate annually. If the account will have saved $1 million in 20 years, the new principle will have grown to $3.87 million.

401K (Plus Company match)

Employer matching your 401K (retirement contribution) implies that the employer is contributing a specific amount towards your retirement saving plan. The contribution by the employer is dependent on the amount of your annual contribution[28].

Based on the conditions set by your employer's 401K plan, the contribution that you make could be matched by using different methods. The common method is where the employer matches the percentage that the employee makes to the 401K plan up to a specific amount of your salary.

The employer may also opt to match your contribution up to a certain dollar quantity. This matching is done irrespective of the compensation you get.

---

[27] Ibid

[28] Claire, B, 2019, *How 401K Matching Works.* <available at>https://www.investopedia.com/articles/personal-finance/112315/how-401k-matching-works.asp

Why Match Your 401K Contribution?

It is important to appreciate that the conditions of the 401K plan differ widely depending on the employer. Other than the standard requirement for contribution and withdrawal as required under the Employee Retirement Income Security Act (ERISA), your employer is free to set the conditions for 401k[29].

The employer could opt to use a generous method or a more stringent one. No matter the method that the employer uses, you have to appreciate that it is free money topped on your retirement benefit savings. Therefore, make sure to grab it!

How the Matching Operates

Assume that your employer is making a 100% match on the contribution that you make annually, to a maximum of 3% annual income. If your salary is $60,000 per year, the employer will contribute $1,800. You will also be required to contribute $1,800 to the retirement plan in order to get the marching benefit.

A more common marching scheme preferred by employers is the model that offers 50% matches of employee contribution that equals 6% of the yearly earning. This means that if your annual salary is $60,000, the employer is eligible to contribute $3,600 for marching. But he will only contribute $1,800 because the marching benefit is capped at 50%. In this case, you will be required to contribute $3,600 in order to get full employer matching benefit.

The Contribution Limits

Irrespective of whether the payments to your 401k plan are being done by you or employer matching, the deferrals have to follow the annual contribution limit set by the Internal Revenue Service (IRS). For example, the contributions by employers in 2019 to all 401k accounts of the same employees were capped at 56,000 or 100% compensation (whichever comes first).

---

[29] Claire, B, 2019, *How 401K Matching Works.* <available at>https://www.investopedia.com/articles/personal-finance/112315/how-401k-matching-works.asp

In the case of elective salary deferrals that are paid by the employees, the limit is capped at $19,000[30].

NOTE: The sum of employer matches does not count towards the employee's deferral limit. Also, you should appreciate that the limits could be updated every year (commonly done around October -November).

Vesting

Besides regularly reviewing your 401K matching needs, it is also prudent to check on vesting schedules. This schedule dictates the level of ownership for employees to the employer's contribution depending on the number of years of employment.

Even if the employer has a very attractive matching plan; you might be required to forego some or all contribution in the event of job termination. A common schedule allows you a percentage of the employer's contribution that increases with your tenure. The Bureau of Labor a Statistics gives five years for you to be fully vested.

The Roth IRA – Your secret retirement weapon

Roth IRA is a unique retirement account that provides tax benefits such as tax-free growth of personal investment. However, not all people qualify for this investment.

Roth IRA encourages people to save progressively by providing tax-related benefits. Unlike the preceding scheme that used to tax investors' savings, money in the Roth IRS plan is tax-free. This implies that the Roth IRA withdrawal that you make later in retirement will be tax-free[35].

The Roth IRA is considered an account that holds the investors' funds as opposed to investment itself. The accounts are opened through brokers and you will be required to select where you want your funds to be directed to. The main options include exchange-traded funds (ETFs), bonds, socks, and mutual funds.

[30] Ibid

Are You Eligible for Roth IRA?

One thing that you will find vexing about Roth IRA is that you will not be eligible if your income is high. Starting from 2019, the rules of investing in Roth IRA were changed. Now, the amount that you can contribute to Roth IRA starts to shrink when it hits certain thresholds that are adjusted based on your growing income. For example, the maximum contribution of a married couple is $6,000[31]. The contribution continues to shrink as the income rises until you reach a point and it is halted.

It is also important to note that you can only contribute earned income. This means the income that you earn from being employed or even self-employed. If you get income such as scholarship and fellowship that is taxable, you are also eligible for the Roth IRA.

Other types of income that can allow you to make savings at Roth IRA include taxable differential and military alimony[32].

The earned incomes that cannot be used on the Roth IRA include dividends and interests from other investments, rental property, and revenue from pension schemes. Besides, you will not be allowed to include other types of income like IRA distributions, K-1 income, and Social Security.

Major Benefits of Joining Roth IRA

As an investor, the primary focus should be opportunities that allow you to optimize profits. One way of achieving this is picking opportunities like Roth IRA where your investment is tax-free. Here are other benefits to expect when you start saving in this scheme.

- The amount you contribute does not follow the common minimum distribution model that is used by 401K starting at the age of 70½. This implies that Roth IRA can be effectively used to optimize returns and pass them to beneficiaries[33].
- When you decide to withdraw Roth IRA scheme, no tax or penalty is imposed. The underlying principle of the scheme is that the income that you are using had already been taxed before being directed to the Roth IRA.

---

[31] iBid

[32] Ibid

[33] RothIRA.co.m, 2019, *Roth IRA Limits.* <available at> https://www.rothira.com/roth-ira-limits

- When you reach year 59½, Roth IRA allows you to take away all the contribution including earnings therein. Note that no federal taxes are levied. This is a great boost for people who are starting or entering retirement.
- The Roth IRA money can be used to pay for college expenses without attracting a penalty. This is very helpful in making your college life smooth[34].
- The plan allows people of all ages to participate. As long as you have income that is allowed on the Roth IRA and you pay taxes, it is a great point to start building your savings.

Mutual funds and ETFs

Mutual funds and Exchange traded funds (ETFs) are funds that consist of different types of assets and present investors with a great way of diversifying their portfolios. They are created from pool fund investing that is designed to help investors enjoy economies of scale. They also allow managers to lower transaction costs through shared transactions using pooled investing capital.

Both ETFs and Mutual funds have many individual securities and are regulated by the Securities Act of 1933, Securities Exchange Act of 1934, and the Investment Company Act of 1990. These laws were designed with the target of lowering the risk of a possible market crash like that of 1929.[35]

One key difference between the two funds is that mutual funds are traditionally designed to provide a wide range of choices while ETFs help to track an index. Here is a closer look at the two.

Mutual Funds

This is a type of managed investment that was first used in the US in 1924. Since then, they have become some of the most preferred investment options for offering investors an

[34] Ibid

[35] Birdthistle, W, and Morney, J, 2018, *Research Handbook on the Regulation of Mutual Funds.* New York: Edward Edgar Publishing.

extensive selection of pooled funds investment[36]. Note that though some are managed passively, the most preferred are those actively managed by top professionals.

As an investor, active management is an important parameter for helping to optimize the portfolio and returns.

It is important to note that actively managed mutual funds attract a high fee because the managers have to identify the best securities on behalf of the investor. The operational fee is expressed as a ratio that includes operational expenses, management fees, and 12B-1 fees. The 12B-1 fee is used to support expenses related to selling the fund via full-service brokerage. Notably, this fee is not charged in ETFs.

ETFs

ETFs started trading in 1993 and are, by law, required to be managed passively using securities tracking as an index. However, the US started allowing actively managed ETFs from 2008.

Traditionally, ETFs were very popular for index operators (traders) who targeted getting exposure to a specific segment of a market. Such traders mainly intended to diversify their portfolios. ETFs have evolved over time and yielded additional options such as the smart beta index funds.

When investing in ETFs, it is important to consider the associated fees. Though investors do not pay a sales load fee, they are required to remit a commission for trading them. Because ETFs are managed passively, the management fee is relatively low. As indicated earlier, ETFs do not charge 12b-1 fees. One outstanding ETF in the market is SPY.

SPY

Spy was created in January 1993 by State Street Global Advisors and became the first ETF to get listed in the US. It grew rapidly and became one of the top trading vehicles based on traded volume in the United States. The traded volume of the vehicle is about 80 million[37].

---

[36] Anthan, N, 2016, Exchange-traded Funds and the New Dynamics of Investing. Oxford: Oxford University Press.

[37] Anthan, N, 2016, Exchange-traded Funds and the New Dynamics of Investing. Oxford: Oxford University Press.

Traders hold SPY in high regard since it represents a group of 500 top US companies (S&P 500 Index) with total capitalization of more than five billion.

Each stock in the S&P 500 Index is required to be actively traded on its own. For investors, the tag (S&P 500 Index) is preferred because it offers better exposure to more companies with a single purchase.

Why Consider Investing in SPY?

The S&P 500 ETF is seen as an easy method for investors and traders to get access to the index that was initially only accessible to those who traded S&P 500 futures before the idea of SPY was created. However, it is important to appreciate that SPY offers more than simply access to an index. Indeed, a lot of ETFs offer access to index but operate way below SPY.

The longevity associated with SPY has made it to easily win the trust of fund managers (State Street). Indeed, traders are willing to trade on a daily basis because they are assured of high volumes that make it easy to open and close trades.

How does SPY Operate?

The S&P 500 works as a unit of trust. State Street buys and sells stocks to help align its pool holding in line with the S&P 500 index. This implies that when you purchase a SPY share, you are simply acquiring a unit that represents the stock of every S&P 500 index.

When investors purchase SPY, their anticipation is that the entire S&P 500 index value will go up. This means that investors can also sell their SPY units on the market at a profit. Note that if the holdings in the fund fall, the value of every SPY will also decline.

It is important to point that for day traders, the focus is not so much whether the index value will shift up or down. Because the S&P 500 stocks move the whole day, tracking SPY is a worthy undertaking. When the small movements are combined with large volumes, day traders capitalize on them to make profits.

Because SPY is traded on the stock market, a trader can decide to buy or sell some shares to or from other interested traders. Note that in some cases, the price of SPY might be too small to cause a major shift in the overall value of the S&P 500 index. However, fear or euphoria can make participants to push the price to record high or low.

If you want to know the actual value of SPY, make sure to check the symbol "SPY.NV every morning.

A Practical Sample Budget When Saving for Retirement

Learning to budget correctly is an important step to help you achieve financial freedom. The primary goal should be ensuring that you understand all the expenses and allocate them ample resources. Here is a sample budget:

Let assume that you are 30 years old and earning an annual income of $150,000 (12,500 monthly). This sample also assumes that you have made zero savings so far and target to retire at 65 years. Besides, you also target to live on 85% of the pre-retirement after retiring (this translates to $42,000).

To hit your goal, a total of $2 million will be needed by the time you retire. Though this could appear like it is a lot of money, it is not because it is spread over 35 years. Here is a breakdown of the budget.

Personal Budget for $12,500 for the month of March 2019	
Category (item)	Allocated Cost Per Item
1. Food 2. Retirement scheme (401K) 3. Roth IRA 4. Emergency fund 5. Student Loan 6. Transport 7. Holiday 8. Family shopping 9. New furniture 10. New television 11. Gifts 12. Personal savings	$3,000 $600 $50 $500 $600 $1,000 $6,00 $2,000 $800 $400

13. Miscellaneous	$300 $1,500 $650
	Total=$12,500

Housing versus Stock Market – the Truth

When people think of investment, two common options that click into their minds are Stocks and Housing. However, which is better between the two? Here is a comparison that seeks to demystify the benefits of each to help you pick the better option.

Real Estate

When you decide to invest in Real Estate, it implies that you are purchasing land or property. Note that some real estate options such as blank parcels of land could cost you more in property taxes even if no income is being generated.

Some properties that can generate cash for you include apartments, strip malls, and rental units. You could also purchase property for improvement and sell later at a profit.

Pros and Investing in Real Estate

- Real estate is a comfortable option to invest in because you have always lived in a house. Therefore, you are conversant with some aspects of housing.
- When you channel resources to real estate, you will get something tangible. This sense of attachment allows you to stand a short distance away and say "that is my house".
- It is not easy to get defrauded when investing in properties because the process of ownership exchange is clearly defined. For example, transactions are completed by real estate attorneys or expert realtors.
- Properties provide you with full control over the investment. Whether you want to improve the houses, introduce new features, or even adjust the prices, you are the boss.

Cons of Real Estate

- Even if the property is not occupied, real estate will still attract some cost such as maintenance and property taxes.
- The return on real estate is very low. After inflation, you can be left with as little as 0% because of the high costs associated with maintaining the venture. For example, you need to meet property taxes, insurance, utilities, maintenance, and toilet drains among others[38].
- You have to struggle with the management to sustain the real estate in top condition. If you prefer to hire a real estate manager, you will have to pay a fee (about 10% of the collected revenue).
- The process of acquiring or disposing of real estate investment is complex and lengthy. For example, you have to search for the preferred property, make physical visits, do a pre-purchase inspection, and wait for a couple of days before property lawyers can complete the transfer.

Stock Markets

Investing in stocks involves buying shares of selected companies and waiting to get a portion of the profit that they generate. It implies that whether the company of choice sells furniture, manufactures cars, deals with video games or offers tax services, you become part of it. For example, if a company has one million shares and you purchase 10,000, you own 1% of the firm.

Pros of Investing in Stock Markets

- Investing in stock markets has been demonstrated for more than 100 years to be a great method of creating wealth. Even though the stock markets have undergone major depressive periods such as the infamous Stock Market Crash of 1929, they easily spring back to offer profits to investors.
- When you buy stocks of a company, you are entitled to getting a share of the generated profit without getting directly involved. This implies that you can purchase the shares and only come back at the end of the year to check the profit they have generated. You will not be required to get directly involved with the management.

---

[38] Rami, S, 2018, *Real Estate Investing: The Myths, facts, and ways to get started.* <available at> https://www.iwillteachyoutoberich.com/blog/surprising-real-estate-investing-myths/

- Apart from the cost of buying the shares, there are no additional expenses. Unlike the real estates that will require some maintenance costs even when no income is generated, stock markets are stress-free.
- Investing in stock markets is very easy. Indeed, you can follow the performance of a company and buy its shares online at the comfort of your home. Besides, you can also sell the shares within minutes.
- If you select high-quality stocks, they will generate both profit and dividends at the end of the year. Take the case of Johnson & Johnson that started trading in 1944. If you bought one share when in 1944 when the cost was $37.50 and held it to date, the value would have gone up an impressive 17%.
- With stocks, it is very easy to diversity. For example, you can invest directly in companies that are performing well in the market or other high return ventures such as mutual funds. Mutual funds allow you to invest as little as $100 per month and rake in huge profits.
- Like real estate, you can borrow cash against your stocks. The only thing that is needed is approval from your trading broker.

Cons of Capital Markets

- Though stocks promise high returns, they can experience extreme fluctuations, especially in the short term. Therefore, it is advisable to only invest in top companies and diversifying your funds onto different types of stocks such as mutual funds, ETFs and stocks.
- When you purchase stocks, you do not have something tangible to associate with. This means that though you own part of a major company, it is not possible to stand there and say this is my company.
- Though you are part of a selected company after buying its shares, you do not have control over it. Instead, the company operates under different management that manages the daily operations.

Though both real estate and stock markets have unique benefits, stocks provide a better option to rake in more revenue. They are also easy to acquire, diversify, and even dispose.

Chapter Eight: Making Credit Cards Work for you

Credit cards are some of the most used methods of payment in the United States today. They are preferred by many people because they are widely accepted in many stores and you can pay without having to carry cash in a wallet.

A lot of people also like the cards because they can spend more than they have. This makes credit card a reliable tool for shopping during emergencies or when you have financial shortfalls. Even with these advantages, credit cards have become like a trap that funnels people to debts. It is estimated that more than 22% of Americans have more credit card debts than savings[39].

This chapter takes a closer look at credit cards to establish how to make them work for you. It explores how the credit card companies make money, and how you can build your credit score. Finally, it outlines the common credit cards in the market that you should consider using today.

How Credit Card Companies Make Money

The large number of Americans with credit card loans leads to one key question: "How do credit card companies generate revenue?" Before looking at the method used by credit card companies to make money, it is important to understand how they work.

Credit card companies comprise of two types of enterprises; networks and issuers.

- Issuers: These are credit unions and banks that issue the credit cards. This means that when you use a credit card, you are simply borrowing cash from an issuer. Even retail credit cards that come with the name of a specific brand such as gas station or merchant are still issued by banks that have entered into a contract with the respective retailer[40].
- Networks: These are companies that process transactions done via credit cards.

---

[39] Megan, E, 2017, *15 Scary Facts about Debt that Should Alarm you*. <available at> https://www.cheatsheet.com/money-career/facts-about-debt-may-alarm-you-today.html/

[40] Abel, G, 2018, Amazing Credit Repair: Boost Your Credit Score, Use Loopholes (Section 609), and Overcome Credit Card Debt Forever. New York: CreateSpace Independent Publishing Platform

Major networks in the United States today include Visa and American Express. However, Discover and American Express are both issuers and networks.

When you make payments using a credit card, it is relayed via multiple parties. The transaction is initiated by the issuer, via the network and finally to the merchant bank. Therefore, the network has to ensure that every transaction is linked to the right card holder.

Credit card companies make money in three key ways: interest, fees, and interchange.

Interest

Most of the credit card companies make their cash from interest payments. It is possible to avoid interest on your credit card by ensuring that the balance is paid on time and in full. However, the interest can accrue when it is carried from one month to another.

Interchange

When you used a credit card for payment, the accepting store has to pay a processing fee that is equivalent to the percentage of the involved transaction. A portion of this fee is credited to the credit card issuer using the payment network. It ranges between 1% and 3% and is referred to as an interchange fee. The fee is set by the network and varies depending on the involved volume and value of the transaction.

Fees

Subprime credit card issuers that specialize with clients who have bad credit make the bulk of their money from fees compared to interests. However, mass-market credit card issuers have a wide range of fees including the following:

- **Annual fee:** This fee is charged on cards that have high reward rates and people with poor credit scores.
- **Cash advance fees:** This fee is charged by issuers when clients use their cards to withdraw funds from ATM. The fee is approximately 3.5% of the cash being withdrawn.
- **Balance transfer fee:** This fee is charged when you transfer debt from one card to another. The interest ranges from 3% to 5% of the amount that you transfer.
- **Late fees:** If you do not pay the minimum amount by the right date, a later charge

fee will be attached to your card.

Building Your Credit Score without Falling into Debt

A credit score is a three digit number that is used to describe how likely a person is to repay a debt. The score is used by lenders and banks when making decisions about the loans to approve or decline[41].

The score is calculated by three credit reporting agencies, Equifax, TransUnion, and Experian based on your financial operations. The agencies work with lenders and companies that you do business with to gather information to use when calculating your credit score. Here are the different types of information that the credit reporting agencies use to calculate your score:

- Your payment history
- The length of time you have had credit
- The amount of debt that you have
- How you are using credit limits
- Type of credit that you have (example, mortgage, student loan, and credit cards among others)

How to Build Your Credit Score without Getting into Debt

When you improve your credit score, you will not be looked at as a high-risk party by financial institutions and other companies that use the score to offer specific services. You will even enjoy lower interest rates on the loans provided to you. Here are the top methods that you should use to strengthen credit score without getting into debt.

- **Pay credit card balance in full.** Because credit score assesses your ability to manage debt, it is important to maintain good record of timely payments. Make sure you understand your credit card balance and pay it in full without letting it overflow to the next month. Note that this will also save you interest charges.

[41] Credit Karma, 2019, *How to Understand Credit score.* <available at> https://www.creditkarma.com/credit-scores/

- **Consider credit cards like debit cards.** One risk associated with credit cards is that your bank account balance does not change when you process payment in a store. It only changes when you pay the credit card bill. Therefore, it is easy to lose track of the amount you are spending.

To avoid this scenario, you need to maintain a budget indicating when to use the card and when not to. If you know how much the card allows you to spend, treat it like a debit card.

- **Leverage credit card options.** Leveraging the credit card is used to help strengthen the credit score and avoid the pitfalls that can pull it down. First, you should carefully manage your debt-to-credit ratio. It is advisable to keep the debt below 30% of the available credit line.

You can also go for credit transfer. This is a good option when you are trying to pay your credit card balance. Transferring balance will help you to clear balance easily and improve the debt-to-credit ratio.

- **Keep Your Credit Card for a Long Time.** Keeping your credit card over a long period especially if it has good standing will help to pull the score up.

Factors that can Damage Your Credit Score

A credit score is perhaps the most important thing about your finances because it determines your ability to access credit from financial institutions. Even if you have a good business idea and want to bridge the financial gap through a bank loan, the request might be turned away if the credit score is poor. Here are the different things that can damage (pull down) your credit score:

- **Missing your loan repayment:** If you are late to repay your loan by more than 30 days, you will be reported to the credit reference bureaus such as Equifax. Then, your credit score will be recalculated and pulled down factoring the late repayment.
- **Requesting too many credit card reports:** Though requesting a credit card report is important to identify errors and getting them corrected, multiple requests gives the impression that you are desperate for credit. This will pull down the credit score.
- **Bankruptcy:** If you are declared bankrupt, your credit score will fall with a huge

margin. It can drop by up to 240 points. Besides, bankruptcy can stay on the report for more than 10 years[42].

- **Tax lien:** If you have an unpaid tax debt, it will damage your credit score by a huge margin of up to 240 points.
- **Debt consolidation:** When you apply for debt consolidation, it implies that you are unable to service all your lines of credit. It will pull down the credit score with a significant margin.
- **Credit report errors:** If your credit report contains errors such as wrong entries or missing information about your financial details, the credit score is likely to be incorrect.

Important Steps for Rebuilding/building Your Credit Score

If your credit score gets damaged by things such as late loan repayment or even bankruptcy, it is very important to consistently rebuild it. Here are useful tips you can use:

- **Start by checking your credit report and correcting errors.** One thing you need to appreciate is that credit reporting agencies that calculate your score rely on the info provided to them by other parties like banks. Therefore, if they have the wrong information or some reports are missing, the credit score will be incorrect[43]. So, you should always start by checking the credit report for errors and having them corrected immediately.

Note that you do not have to pay to get a credit report. Every 12 months, you are entitled to get a free copy of your credit report from AnnualCreditReport.com.

- **Use a Secured credit card:** If you use a standard credit card, controlling spending can be an uphill task. This could easily get you into debts and pull down the credit score. Instead, you should consider going for a secured credit card. This is a type of credit card that requires you to make an upfront deposit to prevent overspending.

---

[42] Baverley, Harzog, 2015, The Debt Escape Plan: How to Free Yourself From Credit Card Balances, Boost Your Credit Score, and Live Debt-Free. Washington: Red Wheel Weiser.

[43] Baverley, Harzog, 2015, The Debt Escape Plan: How to Free Yourself From Credit Card Balances, Boost Your Credit Score, and Live Debt-Free. Washington: Red Wheel Weiser.

This is a great way to stay within your budget and rebuild credit score.

- **Pay your bills on time:** There is a general perception that it is only bank credit and mortgage that can be reported to the credit reporting agencies. But this is wrong. If you fail to pay your power, water and gas bills on time, they can also pull down the score. Therefore, you should always ensure that such bills are paid on time.
- **Keep old financial accounts active:** It is advisable to be smart with credit cards by avoiding closing the card accounts. When your report has a higher average age on the credit card accounts, the credit score will go up. It is also advisable to avoid opening many credit cards within a short time because it can be interpreted that you are eager for credit.
- **Try to maintain the same level of activity with your card:** If your credit card is inactive or gets closed, it will push down the credit score. Instead, you should keep the credit cards active even if you only use it to make minimum purchases to keep it on.
- **Ensure to prudently manage your finances:** Even as you use the credit card to rebuild your credit score, it is important to appreciate that even activities in other areas such as student loan or medical credit can still push it down[44]. Therefore, manage your finances prudently to avoid falling into debts that can suddenly pull down the score. It is especially crucial to ensure you have emergency funds to cater for unexpected occurrences such as medical emergencies. Make sure that your family also has medical insurance coverage. Now that you know how to build your credit score using a credit card without falling into debt, it is also important to have the right cards. Here are the main types of credit cards you should consider.

1) **Citi Double Card:** This card offers 2% cash back on every single purchase that you make. It is considered the best cash back card on the market because it does not have revolving categories or annual fees.
2) **Amex Blue Cash Preferred**: This card charges annual fee of $75 per year, but offers 6% cash back on the groceries (with a cap), 3% on gas stations, and 1% on everything else. This card can be a great option for families that spend a lot on groceries and gas.

[44] Ibid

Chapter Nine: Side Hustles & Making Money Online

One question that might be lingering at the back of the mind is; "How can I reach financial freedom fast?" One of the answers to the question is creating multiple sources of passive income. The additional revenue can be used to knock down your debts fast, build savings, and even expand your business.

This chapter demonstrates how to make streams of income and explores different methods you can use to make money online. As you look for investment opportunities, the chapter also demonstrates how to spot and avoid pyramid schemes.

What is Passive Income and Multiple Streams of Revenue?

The concepts of passive income and multiple streams of revenue are important when working towards financial freedom. Passive income is income that you generate on a regular basis but with minimum effort to maintain it.

Having multiple streams of revenue especially, of passive income, is very important when building wealth. Whether you are at your workplace or home, the different streams of revenue keep funneling money to your portfolio.

The main reason for creating passive income is because it is not connected to your time. This implies that you can still be engaged in doing other tasks such as creating new streams of income.

One thing that you need to appreciate about passive income is that it does not need to be a lot of money. The little you can make will go a long way to helping grow your finances. Think of a passive line of income that generates $500 a month. Though it might look small, it could go a long way to help build long term savings.

In a year, your $500 will have reached $6,000 which could be enough to clear part of your student loan, mortgage or other debt. Indeed, if your debt requires you to only pay $500 or less per month, the passive income could cater for it so that your main income can go into other areas such building new businesses or an emergency fund.

Three Steps to Creating Multiple Streams of Passive

Revenue

To create multiple streams of revenue, here are three proven steps that you should consider.

1. Start by Picking One Stream of Revenue You are Passionate about

The first stream of revenue should be something that you love. This is because the first stream of revenue could be the toughest since you had not been engaged in a similar venture before[45].

Note that you might need to take time learning about the stream of revenue. Depending on the selected channel, it might be important to start by setting the parameters of operations such as the services on sale, the audience, and the targeted niche.

By selecting a stream that you are passionate about, it implies that you can wait until the income starts flowing. If the first stream of income works for you, it might be possible to diversify to others.

2. Systemize the First Stream of Income

After perfecting the first stream of revenue, go ahead and systematize it so that only your limited attention and time will be needed. This is done by using appropriate human resources and technologies. You are simply leaving other people or automating the system so that you can concentrate on creating new streams of income.

Before you can fully hand over, make sure to pre-test the new team or automation to get the assurance that operations will run effectively and create the targeted revenue.

3. Leverage Resources to Create Additional Streams of Income

Once the first stream of income starts generating revenue without taking much of your time, then you will now have ample time and energy to build the next stream of income. The skills and knowledge that you gained in the first stream of revenue are crucial when building the next source of income.

---

[45] The Financial Mentor, 2019, *Multiple Streams of Revenue: The Truth Revealed.* <available at>https://financialmentor.com/wealth-building/wealth-program-system/multiple-streams-of-income/13096

Because you took time learning how the first stream of income works, you will not need to start from scratch when working on new streams. If you create an online application and design a website to sell it, it will be easier to market newer apps because you could still use the same site. Creating newer streams of revenue will be easier and faster compared to the first one.

Opportunities you can exploit to make Passive Income

Today, there are many opportunities that you can exploit to add new streams of revenue to your financial portfolio. Here are some of them:

1. ***Affiliate Marketing***

Affiliate marketing is a performance-based type of marketing where a business uses affiliates to market its product. Then, the affiliate marketer is paid a commission when a client he brings buys the product under consideration[46]. It is a cheap way for you to start making money online without creating your own product.

How Does Affiliate Marketing Work?

To be successful as an affiliate marketer, you need to identify a niche of interest and build a large following. You can do this by establishing yourself as an authority to win a large and loyal following. This can also be achieved through writing content about the niche of interest and engaging the community to win its trust.

Once you have created a loyal following, you will need to select a good Affiliate Marketing program such as WordPress Affiliate Manager or Shortlinks. These programs help to track your performance and carefully follow clients who purchase after your persuasion.

It is also important to set your affiliate marketing channels where you can recommend products to your followers. This means your website and marketing email list. You can also install third-party plugins such as Post Affiliate Pro and ShareSale to help you to evaluate the level of success.

[46] Marketing Artfully, 2019, How to add affiliate marketing as a revenue stream <available at>https://marketingartfully.com/add-affiliate-marketing-revenue-stream/

Useful Tips to Help You Become A Pro Affiliate Manager

One fact you need to appreciate when starting an affiliate marketing program is that it is not a get-rich-overnight venture. Today, affiliate marketing has become highly competitive. Therefore, you need to carefully build your portfolio to win the trust of both followers and businesses. Here are some useful tips to help you succeed in affiliate marketing.

- **It is advisable to only work with a few products:** The first mistake that you can make in affiliate marketing is picking too many products or trying to promote everything. The problem with this approach is that you are likely to get overwhelmed. Instead, you should only pick a few items that you can easily promote and convince your followers to purchase.
- **Use multiple traffic sources for product promotion:** In many cases, affiliate marketers only put the ads on their sites and blogs. But this is the wrong way to do it because people who are not visiting your site are likely to miss the ads.

The ideal marketing method is reaching the target audience via multiple channels. You should particularly maintain a presence on the top social media pages such as Facebook and Instagram. Other channels include your blog, YouTube, and Guest pages.

- **Make sure to comprehensively research the demand of the target product:** Though you want to make money via affiliate marketing, you cannot simply pick any item because the manufacturer has placed a request. To know the right product to promote, you need to research its demand.

Take a bit of your time analyzing the product's demand. The goal is picking an item that is easy to market instead of a product that is likely to get rejected. Ensure to follow the product development process and also tie it with the image of the manufacturer.

- **Aim at strengthening your followers' base:** Even though the primary target of affiliate marketing is creating additional income, it is important to look at the venture from a long term perspective. Though you are recommending products of other companies, try to maintain buyers as part of your community.

To build a lasting community, the focus should be providing the correct status of the items you recommend as opposed to simply market it. If you find that a product is lacking in one way or another, decline marketing it. This honesty will ensure that you always have huge following and products to market.

Pros of Affiliate Marketing

- No investment is needed to create your own products
- There is a wide range of products to be promoted
- Customer service is the role of the businesses seeking your affiliate marketing services
- It is a high-income potential channel
- Allows you to sell complementary products simultaneously. For example, you can sell your own products and those of the contracting businesses

Cons of Affiliate Marketing

- You lack control over a lot of things in the marketing process. These include product features, updates, and price.
- Building a trustworthy following is not easy. It could take months or even years.

2. ***Blogging***

Blogs were originally created as platforms for helping brands build communities and making regular communications with the target audience. However, they have evolved to become top marketing platforms for businesses and individuals. Here is an account of how you can create a new stream of revenue through blogging.

Identify a Blogging Niche

Even before you can set up a blog, it is important to pick up one or several niches that you want to blog about. This will help to present yourself as an expert and mold you into an authority over time[47].

To pick the right niche, it is advisable to pick the area you are passionate about. For example, if you have an interest in fitness, consider blogging on niches such as weight

[47] ProBlogger, 2017, *Make Money Blogging.* <available at> https://problogger.com/make-money-blogging/

management and fitness training. Other areas of consideration can be human resources management, pregnancy, early childhood development, and education.

After selecting the preferred niche, start researching it to understand the target audience, its preferences, and other players. This will help you to craft a winning approach to draw high traffic and create interest from companies.

Create Your Blogging Platform

Now that you have decided about the area of interest, you need to create a blog. This is a platform just like a website but that is mainly used for communication and liaison with the target audience. Though you could engage a web developer to create a winning blog, it is also possible to create one from scratch.

Top Content Management System (CMS) platforms such as WordPress allow you to create a new blog from scratch in just a few clicks. They have multiple templates that come with most features such as content publishing and search engine optimization (SEO) that will come in handy once your blog starts running.

You will also need to host your blog using companies such as GoDaddy and HostGator. Ensure to pick the hosting provider that guarantees fast loading and high uptime of more than 99.99%. Note that the hosting provider will also charge a small fee for hosting the blog. The average hosting cost today is about $2.5/ month.

Start Creating and Publishing Content on Your Blog

Now that your blog is live, you need to start creating content to draw traffic and build a community. Most of the people visiting your blog will be looking for engaging content that educates, entertains, and guides them. Therefore, it is important to interact with the target audience and understand what it wants.

Your content should be comprehensively researched to progressively build you as an authority in the niche. Make sure to target different areas of the selected niche and post content regularly to keep the audience coming back for more.

Note that once the blog starts running, it will not be enough to drive traffic on its own. You need to share it and the content with other websites, blogs, and social media platforms. This will help to draw a lot of traffic to the blog. When the blog following grows to thousands, companies will start developing an interest in reaching them.

Start Making Money Online

Just like in affiliate marketing, it is important to appreciate that blogging requires ample time to start generating income. Therefore, the main goal should be building an engaged audience that views you as an authority. Then, use the following strategies to generate revenue:

- **Make income from advertising:** This is the starting point for most bloggers' website monetization. Because of the large following coming to your blog, you will be viewed as a perfect point for companies to place advertisements. Now, you can charge them based on the nature and time of the ad.
- **Start generating affiliate income:** Now that you have a loyal following, you could create another stream of revenue via affiliate marketing. Here, you will be marketing products from other companies to your audience and getting paid some commission when your referrals make purchases.
- **Run events and charge a fee:** Though advertising is the main line of revenue for most bloggers, holding events can help raise even more income. Running online events such as conferences at specific intervals and charging attendants a fee can generate a lot of revenue.

The good thing with blogging events is that they can be attended by viewers from across the world. This implies that you are not restricted by administrative boundaries and, therefore, can generate a lot of income.

- **Develop recurring income with the blog:** Because most of your followers come to read content, you can create a channel of recurring income by creating membership programs. The members are allowed to access top-notch content, tools, or a combination of services for a monthly or annual cost. Note that this stream of income revenue would require you to also generate high-quality content for the members.
- **Create own products to sell on the blog:** If you are an expert in a specific area, you can generate a product such as a guide, app or ebook and sell to the followers.

For example, a fitness enthusiast can sell an ebook guide for cutting weight and staying healthy. Though such ebooks take time to create, they can generate a lot of income over time.

Pros of Blogging

- Provides high potential for making a lot of money
- You can create multiple streams of revenue using blogging
- It requires a limited amount of money to set up and start generating money
- You can also sell own digital products and services such as ebooks, guides, tools, and applications

Cons of Blogging

- Logging requires a lot of time to create and start earning a lot of money. First, you have to build yourself as an authority and drive a huge following
- Today, blogging has become very competitive. This makes it even harder to outdo competitors and start earning the cash you want

3. *Self-Publishing Books*

In the past, thoughts of making a publication were complex and, seemingly, out of reach for many people. However, the emergence of self-publishing platforms like Amazon has now made it easy for you to write a book of choice and publish it for millions of viewers across the globe to read. Think of this as a unique opportunity to reach millions of readers and sell them your book.

To start making money on Amazon, you need to sign up for a free Kindle Direct Publishing (KDP) account that allows you to create and add new books within minutes. The account simply requires you to fill the title of the book, author name, cover, description, the book price, and the book before clicking publish. Then, your book will be reviewed in about 24 hours before getting published.

When Amazon sells your book, it pays you a royalty of 70%. Here is a complete guide on how to make money through self-publishing books on Amazon:

Identify a Profitable Category

To make money publishing books at Amazon, you only need to look for areas that attract a lot of interest. Think of your area of interest such as fitness, employment, value addition, money management, and relationships. You could even start by exploring the challenges facing the targeted audience and create a book to address them.

It is important to appreciate that as a self-publishing portal, the competition is very high. Therefore, getting a high-value niche with low competition can be your gateway to generating a lot of income.

Evaluate the Profitability of the Book Ideas

One mistake that you should avoid making is assuming that there is a ready market for whatever book you publish on Amazon. Before you can start creating the book of interest, it is important to carry comprehensive research on Amazon and other platforms such as Google Books. For example, you can simply search the title of the book you want to write on the Amazon Kindle to see similar works with the same ideas.

Create Your Book Title and Cover

After choosing a niche of interest, the next step should be coming up with a title and book cover. Make sure to have a catchy keyword included in the title so that clients searching for related info can easily pick it. If your primary keyword is something like "acne treatment", a good title could be "*Acne Treatment-The Simple, Tested, and Proven Ways to Cure Acne Fast.*"

Write your Book and Publish

Now that you have the right niche, the right title, and an Amazon Kindle account, it is time to get down and write the book. Make sure to carefully present the ideas so that readers will find the book enjoyable to read. This way, they will even recommend it to colleagues and friends.

You can also hire other people to write the book on your behalf. This is a great way to handle high-value topics that are out of your area of specialization. Consider checking for freelance writers on top writing platforms such as Upwork and WarriorForum.

Once the book is ready, it is time to publish it so that readers can see, buy, and read. To get more people to read the book, you should consider giving it away to a number of people and ask them to leave reviews.

Pros of Self-Publishing Books on Amazon

- Fast exposure of your content
- High potential for a lot of revenue
- Longer shelf life of your books
- The process of publishing is easy once you complete a book

Cons of Self-Publishing Books on Amazon

- There is less editorial and marketing support.

4. *Private Labeling with Amazon FBA*

Private labeling is one of the new methods that could generate a lot of money for you. It is a business model where you sell products on Amazon under your own label. Once you have studied a product of interest and market, you simply go ahead and contact the manufacturer to produce it and sell on Amazon under your brand name[48]. This is awesome.

Many people like the idea of being able to market different products under their labels because they can operate like big stores and make a lot of profit without leaving their house. To make more through private labeling, it is advisable to select a product that has a lot of demand.

Pros of Private Labeling

- You are allowed to sell any product on the giant Amazon e-commerce website
- You do not have to worry about product production
- Private labeling has huge potential for high income

Cons of Private Labeling

- You do not have direct control over the product content such as taste and dimensions

---

[48] Randy, B, 2017, *Your Amazon Label Guide for Passive Income, Part 1.* <available at> https://medium.com/@randybechtold/your-amazon-fba-private-label-guide-for-passive-income-part-1-eb5b53a031c6

Economies of Scale of digital vs physical products

When deciding on the multiple streams of revenue to consider, you might be wondering whether to sell digital or physical products. The main focus should be the ability to generate as many products as possible and pushing them to the target audience without cost limitations[49].

- **Digital Products:** These are products that exist in an intangible format. The products are highly scalable because once you create one, it can be reproduced into millions of copies at no extra cost. For example, if you create a book to sell online, millions of clients can download it without affecting the original copy.
- **Physical products:** If you opt to sell physical products, the economies of scale will be poor because of the high cost of production. For example, the process of creating a detergent requires physical facilities, human labor, and actual transportation from the manufacturer to the seller[50]. The complex production and supply chains of physical products make it difficult to generate significant revenue.

Because multiple streams of revenue should be able to work effectively without taking a lot of your time, it is advisable to consider dealing with digital products. If you create a book, it can keep generating income for many years without incurring additional costs.

Multi-Level Marketing Traps: How to Spot and Avoid Them

Multi-Level Marketing companies, or in practical terms, pyramid schemes, are "get rich quick" schemes that are run by a small group of people that want to steal from unsuspecting investors. In a common pyramid scheme, this group of scammers is at the "apex of the pyramid"[51].

[49] Mark, G, 2019, *Digital Economies at Global Margins.* Cambridge, Ma: MIt Press.

[50] Ibid

[51] Robert, F, 2019, Ponziomics: The Untold story of Multi-Level Marketing and How Direct Selling Became an American Swindle. New York: FitzPatrick Management Incorporated.

The first pyramid scheme was run by Charles Ponzi who created a "top-down" scam that promised promissory notes of 50% interest in three months to investors. During the scam, Ponzi made $15 million.[52]

- How Do Pyramids Schemes Work

Pyramids commence with an originator who sits at the top of the scheme. He puts a small amount of money into the scheme and advertises it as a great opportunity to make quick money. The idea is to look like the organization is selling a product or service but the primary goal is to convince people to join and charge them a fee.

Because you are promised repayment at a high-interest rate, the new people joining the pyramid provide the cash needed to pay the early investors. The schemes even generate financial accounts, profit statements, and anything that can depict them as genuine operators.

The last moment of a pyramid scheme is when it grows and becomes impossible to pay investors. When the early investors cash out, it becomes impossible to pay those at the bottom of the pyramid[53]. When investors realize there is no cash to pay them, the pyramid simply collapses.

- How to Identify and Avoid MLM Pyramid Schemes

To avoid losing your money through pyramid schemes, you should be able to easily identify them and stay away. Here are some of the indicators to look for:

1. **Look for high-pressure investment environment:** The pyramid initiators and marketers want to make it seem as if you are going to miss a very big opportunity that will never come back in life. The aim of this is making you hand over money without carefully investigating the investment opportunity under consideration.
2. **Being required to sign up via other people:** If you find an investment venture that is requiring you to sign-up via another person, the chances are that it is a pyramid. The person seeking to recruit you has been promised good returns if he

[52] Ibid

[53] Robert, F, 2019, Ponziomics: The Untold story of Multi-Level Marketing and How Direct Selling Became an American Swindle. New York: FitzPatrick Management Incorporated.

introduces new members so that they can pay and keep growing the pyramid.

3. **Pyramid schemes involve selling cheap services or products:** If you take a closer look at the products being sold by the organization and note they are of poor quality and are not sold via the conventional marketing channels like retail lines, the chances are that it is a pyramid scheme[54]. Here, you should ask questions such as; "If the product is so good, has it been approved by relevant authorities?" and "Why is it not common in the market?"
4. **An upfront fee or large capital is required:** If you are required to make a specific initial deposit promising very high returns, it is time to take a moment and think about it. For example, if an investment opportunity promises 50% returns in just a few months; try to ask the nature of the investment with such super returns. When the deal is too good to be true, make sure to think twice.

Popular MLM Companies

- Advocare
- Arbonne
- Monat
- Avon
- Cutco
- DoTERRA
- LuLaRoe
- Lipsense
- Amway
- Young Living
- Mary Kay
- Scentsy
- Rodan + Fields

[54] Robert, F, 2019, Ponziomics: The Untold story of Multi-Level Marketing and How Direct Selling Became an American Swindle. New York: FitzPatrick Management Incorporated.

Conclusion

You do not have to have a lot of money to live a large life. However, being liberated from debts will usher you into a new phase of financial freedom and success. The problem of debt is reeling because people do not take the right approaches to address it. However, you are a powerhouse and can overcome it.

From an early stage in life, people are ushered into the life of debt such that they rarely acknowledge it getting out of control. However, this book has demonstrated that it is possible to emerge from debt and blast through into the millionaire you always wanted to be.

Once you create the right mindset to clear the debt, everything else will start falling into place. You also need to cut unnecessary spending and direct cash to addressing the debt. If you are using the right model such as the 4-step debt eliminator, the process of knocking the debt off will become easier as loans get cleared one at a time.

As you move out of debt, it is important to start creating multiple streams of revenue and investing in different areas. Do not wallow in debts, there is a way out.If you follow the advice in this book over a consistent period of time, you will be in a much better position than 95% of people.

Online Side Hustle

Newbie-Friendly Guide for Making Your First $1,000 in Passive Income Each Month on Autopilot -- With 7 Proven Business Models Including Social Media, Shopify, and Amazon FBA

Written By

Financial Freedom Blueprint

Introduction

As technology pushes new boundaries on a daily basis, people are also becoming more savvy. 2019 is a year of growth, not only with internet-powered industries, but also with people who are seeking independence. Given all the different ways to make money online, both scams and legitimate sources, it can be difficult to know which route to take. This guide is meant to teach you about the most viable ways to make a side income, no gimmicks or pyramid schemes included! In order to succeed in these jobs, all you must provide is a few hours of time each week. There is no need to sell all of your stuff on Craigslist, or start a blog that will never gain traction. In a year where nearly anything is possible at the click of a button, it is time to learn how to make the most of your online presence, and turn your wisdom into an additional income.

Inside the book you'll find 7, proven business models which can have you earning your first $1,000/month online, faster than you could have ever imagined.

Online Marketing Mindset – what it really takes to succeed

The biggest thing that holds people back from making money online isn't a lack of technical skill or knowledge. Most "marketers" will give you the impression that there are a ton of secrets which you need to pay to know.

This isn't really the case. In fact, the biggest thing that holds people back is a lack of understanding about how money and competition works.

Most people have a scarcity mindset when it comes to money. There isn't enough of it, or that it's always running out.

This is what separates the rich from the poor, not intelligence or anything else. The rich have an abundance mindset regarding money, and the poor have a scarcity mindset.

"It's too late to make money online", or "other people are already doing it" are two phrases I hear regularly. These phrases imply there is a finite amount of demand and a finite amount of money in the world. Neither of these are true, and are prime examples of a scarcity mindset.

Ask yourself this, is there just one successful cell phone manufacturer? Absolutely not.

How many brands of beans do you see at the store? More than one, right?

The fact is, there is more than enough demand in the world for anyone to be successful online. Particularly when we're talking about making your first $1,000.

And competition does not mean someone else has already "taken" all the money. Quite the contrary. Competition validates your idea, because people are already making money with it. Which means there is proven demand for what you're doing.

Thousands of people are making a good living (some even 7 or 8 figures a year) with the business models listed inside this book. And yet, there is still more than enough room for you, or anyone else, to come in an get your slice of the pie.

Let's break it down some more with math.

To make $1,000 a month, you need to sell

100 products @ $10

20 products @ 50

10 products @ $100

5 products @ $200

Now, if you have an online store (for example, I searched magnet car mounts, and the first site which came up was the below)

https://themagnetmount.com/

The "Wireless Charging Mount" on here is listed at $70. So the owners only have to sell 15 of these per month to make $1000.

That's one every two days.

When you consider there are 263 million car owners in the US alone. Do you think it'd be that hard to find 15 people willing to buy one? I don't think so.

Now, obviously there is more to it than this simple example, and I will expand on the technical details of each model as we move further on in the book, but I just want to illustrate just how easy it is to make money online in 2019.

So your lesson should be this, adopt an abundance mindset in everything you do. Do that, and the money will flow to you easier than it ever has before.

If you would like to hear more about the idea of abundance mindsets, then there are two main resources I would recommend.

The first is Robert Kiyosaki's classic *Rich Dad, Poor Dad*. You can pick up a copy on Amazon for less than $10.

The second is a lesser known work. *No BS Wealth Attraction in the New Economy* by esteemed marketing legend Dan Kennedy.

I prefer Kennedy's work as I think the practical examples Kiyosaki gives are somewhat dated, and in some cases, counter-productive to his theoretical advice. But both are worthy reads.

But for this book, we will focus more on the practical business models you can use to make your first $1,000 online.

Social Media Marketing

Did you know that thousands of people make money by simply posting on social media? This is one of the top ways to make a side income as a newbie, and you don't even have to leave your home! Essentially, social media marketing can be done anywhere and at any time. It does take a bit of skill and understanding, but once you have it down, it is a super easy way to see quick results. Because so many of us are already on these platforms, it only makes sense to turn it into something profitable; the audience already exists. Whether you like to utilize Facebook, Instagram, Twitter, Tumblr, or all of the above, there are existing opportunities for you to capitalize on.

Finding Your Niche

The work that must be done before you can start seeing results takes a bit of research -- you need to figure out what you are passionate about, and who is willing to listen. As mentioned, the audience is already out there, and it is your job as an influencer to pinpoint it. If you aren't sure which direction you'd like to take your social media accounts in, start by taking a look at the content that already exists. Consider the following factors:

- What kinds of accounts do you like to follow?
- Which of your followers has the most interaction?
- How frequently do your followers post?

This will give you an idea of what kind of accounts are already generating success. It can be a general rule of thumb that adding to a niche that is already thriving will allow you faster results. Your niche can be anything, really. There is an industry for those in the beauty field (hair/makeup/skincare/clothing). If you are into sports, you can utilize this by posting recaps and information about current events. Television shows and movies already have large followings; you can turn this into your own niche, creating an account that will focus on certain events involving the cast or posting reviews. Lifestyle is a huge niche that is currently trending in 2019 -- people like to see how others live, what they eat, and where they travel.

No matter what direction that you choose to go in, your niche will become your own personal brand. People respond well to accounts that are cohesive and consistent. If you start by making three posts a week, commit to this! Your followers are going to be expecting those posts, and if you stop posting for weeks at a time, this is when people will start to lose interest. Engagement is important, and aside from posting regularly, you also want to make sure that you are providing quality content. Think about it this way: Is this post something that you would like to see on your feed? Keep it interesting, and try to avoid filler.

Have an intention behind everything that you post. If you spam your followers with a bunch of filler, it is unlikely that they are going to want to interact with you. They might even become tired of the posts and decide to unfollow you. It is important to generate real engagement from real social media users. Once you have this platform built up, you would be surprised at who will take notice of your accounts. The more followers that you have, the more likely it will be for companies to want to work with you.

Because you probably already have these accounts in place, gaining more followers should not take much time out of your day. You can work on engaging with other users and posting quality content in as little as 5 minutes, right when you open your app. Engagement is anything from liking others' posts to leaving (or responding to) comments. Following similar accounts is also going to help you by building up a network of like-minded individuals.

Sponsorship and Collaborations

Once your follower count is up and you have active users that are interacting with your posts, the exciting part begins. Certain companies and organizations like to collaborate with social media users. Yes, that is correct -- these brands will pay you for simply posting on your social media accounts! It can be hard to determine a starting point at first; brands won't likely reach out to you until you are pretty established, but *you* can start reaching out to *them*. This will show initiative and drive. Paired with your consistent posts and follower engagement, your personal brand should be strong enough to participate in collaborations.

A good way to find these opportunities is to search for brands that are seeking "brand ambassadors." This is a term that describes a group of people who are chosen by a brand to represent it. This type of collaboration usually involves the company sending you their product (either for free or at a discounted rate), and then providing you with your own personal discount code that you can give to your followers. By posting content wearing/using/talking about said brand and offering a discount code, you are essentially generating new business for them.

Companies usually offer a type of commission-based payment rate, and the more sales that you generate for them, the more money that you will earn. As you can probably imagine, this type of collaboration can develop very quickly. Plus, the more that you do these collaborations, the more your engagement and follower statistics will grow.

Once companies see that your numbers are steadily increasing, they might even begin to send you their products for free. As long as they feel that your account and your personal brand is viable, they are still going to be benefiting from the exposure that you provide. Sometimes, brands will tell you a list of key points that they would like you to mention to your followers. When the details are included like this, a contract might also be a part of the deal. This is how sponsored post opportunities begin.

When a brand is sponsoring your post, they might provide you with some money up front (along with the product and a list of what they would like you to say to your followers). Of course, you need to use your common sense as the opportunities begin to arise. Stay true to yourself and your brand by only promoting companies that you actually support, and products that you actually have an interest in. Your followers will know that something is up if you begin promoting dog food on a makeup tutorial social media account, for example.

An alternative way to get noticed is by collaborating with someone who has a steadily rising profile. This can happen in several different ways. One way to get noticed is to tag larger accounts in your posts; make sure that what you are tagging this person in is relevant, because nobody likes spam. Having someone with a lot of followers repost something of yours is a great way to get noticed. Again, genuine interaction is best. Only tag others in content that is relevant and your own if you are trying to collaborate in this way.

As you build your reputation, you can try to message others to see if they would like to do an official collaboration. This can be something like each one making a post on the same topic/idea/theme and then mentioning the other person in the caption. This type of collaboration can be done with anyone; it is a great way to build your network and help out your fellow influencer. The same idea applies to brands as it does to other influencers: The more you collaborate, the more your reputation will grow.

Posting Videos

While a little bit more involved, creating your own videos is a great way to further connect with your followers and grow your brand. For example, if you are into skincare, making videos showing your various skincare routines will help boost your content rating. People like to see genuine content, so always try your best to be yourself in front of the camera. If you start making videos, YouTube is a great platform to grow on. Users on YouTube can utilize pre-placed ads to make money per click. By allowing YouTube to run these ads before/during your video, you will be making money each time a viewer responds to them.

The more you grow on YouTube, the more money you will be able to make. There is also a way to get paid per view on your video. If you notice that your view count is steadily rising, so can your income. There are plenty of resources available online regarding the various ways that you can make money by posting on YouTube. You don't need to have thousands of followers, either. As long as you are posting quality content, viewers will show an interest.

Your videos will become an extension of your social media portfolio. Brands like to see how you are in front of the camera, and might even offer you sponsorship/collaboration opportunities because of it. While posting videos isn't for everyone, if you are passionate about it, it can be worth a shot. Videos take more work than the average social media post. You will need to come up with a relevant idea, think about who your target audience is, and then record, edit, and post.

Once you get the hang of it, you might find that this brings you faster success than traditional social media posts. A common misconception is that you need a bunch of expensive equipment to get started with creating your own visual content. This isn't necessarily true. If you have a phone and a quiet place to film, then you are ready to get started. Think about what you would like to see in a video if you were the audience watching. No fancy gimmicks are needed to produce quality content.

If you are still unsure about getting started, do your own watching for a little while. Search for content that is similar to what you think you'd like to create, and take pointers from those videos. Think about the way that the YouTuber has outlined each video and how the background is set up. You'll probably a notice a pattern, because just the same as with other forms of social media, YouTube also follows certain trends that cater to what the audience wants to see. Notice the way that YouTubers title their videos and what kind of videos are popular in the moment. A lot of free information can be accessed, as long as you are willing to do some research.

Getting a Manager

When influencers gain traction in the industry, it is not uncommon to seek agency management. Getting an agent for your social media posts is the same concept as getting a talent agent. Normally, you must reach a certain level of followers/views before you are able to apply for representation. The rules are generally clear cut, so you should be able to visit the various agency websites to see if you meet the criteria for management. There are several different networks that manage users within the different industries. From makeup tutorials to comedy, you can obtain this representation to further your career in social media.

As mentioned, if you want to get one of these managers, you must be able to obtain a certain number of followers. The agency is going to want to make sure that it is representing an influencer that has what it takes to continue growing in the industry. This also involves signing a contract. Your manager will disclose what percentage is given to the agency vs. what you get paid. While some see this as a downside, others see it as an opportunity to have access to more jobs.

Your manager will apply for certain brand deals and sponsorships on your behalf. It takes a lot of the work out of approaching these companies for you. As long as you have a consistent brand to present, your manager will do the rest. This is how a lot of rising social media personalities take the next step. While you do not have to get representation to succeed in the industry, the option is there for you if you want to grow your brand even more.

Existing Business Ads

If you have an existing business that you would like to promote, you can do this by way of social media. The same rules apply to this type of an account as they do to a personal account. Your business is your brand, and you will want to make sure that you are staying true to your niche. Make sure that you are regularly engaging with your followers, and possibly even run promotions. Example: “Follow us on Instagram for a 15% discount!” You need to be just as savvy with your business account as you are with your own personal account.

A platform for you to run ads on your posts already exists within each app. Normally, you will make a post, and then you will have the option to "boost" or promote it. By doing this, your post will be pushed up higher into the algorithm. Facebook and Instagram have easily integrated ways for you to start doing this. By placing ads on other users news feeds that promote your business, you will generate more interest and potential new clients.

Payment for this type of advertising is usually on a pay-per-click basis. You begin by sorting out your parameters -- Who do you want to see this post? Selecting an age range and location gives you the opportunity to advertise to the exact demographic that you would like as future clients. Each time someone clicks on your ad, you are charged a small fee. When you are first creating your ad, you can select a maximum budget. For example, $20. The platform will take this budget and promote your post accordingly. This means the bigger budget you have to work with, the more the post will be promoted.

You don't have to shell out large amounts of money to advertise your business. Even for as little as a $1 budget, you can advertise. This is the benefit of using social media. You are self-sufficient, selecting exactly which users you would like to see your post. Also, you are not at the liberty of an advertising agency. Traditional business advertising usually involves a middleman and a much larger payment that is due up front.

Working for Others

If maintaining your own social media account does not interest you, getting a job where you represent someone else could be a nice solution. Plenty of people and businesses alike are trying to grow their brands; they are willing to hire others to help them grow. This is a perfect way to earn additional income, because it is usually not a full-time job. If you have a couple of hours to spend on social media each week, you will likely qualify. Finding a job like this could be as simple as offering to help a friend, or as official as searching job postings online. The level that you want to take it is up to you.

Some tasks that you can expect to be asked to do are: coming up with images/captions, making regular posts, liking others' posts, interacting with followers, and trying to get the brand noticed. Because of the way that this technology has developed over the last decade, many older businesses do not really know where to begin. This is where your skills can bridge the gap between old and new. A lot of business owners are grateful to find someone who is already knowledgeable about social media to help run their accounts.

Running social media accounts is also a great way to meet people in various businesses. Befriending your local business owners could come in handy for if you ever need their services or products in the future. A lot of what social media marketing involves is presenting a likable image to the public -- This includes both the brand and yourself. It gives you the chance to be innovative, as well as creative. Many people enjoy this type of work as a side job because it allows the opportunity for more freedom than a traditional job.

A job like this could turn into something more permanent, if you choose. Beyond posting on social media, this type of job delves into the industry of advertising and the skills of being a personal assistant. Ask around -- you'd be surprised which of your friends, or even family members, would be willing to hire you in order to keep their social profiles current.

Selling Your Own Products

Have you ever come up with a business idea, but were unsure of where to begin? Consider social media! Plenty of people use their accounts to promote and sell handmade goods. This is a great platform to utilize for free advertisement. Another good thing about using social media to promote and sell your creations is that you do not need to rent a physical location to make sales. There are also many ways to accept payments via the internet through services such as PayPal, Stripe, and Google Wallet. With technology, so much is possible now that was never possible before.

If you aren't the type of person who enjoys making goods, you can use your social media accounts to promote different skills that you have. If a dancer chooses to post choreography videos on social media, this could lead to a growing personal brand and potential future job opportunities. The more that you are willing to put yourself out there, the better a chance there is of profiting off of your skills or crafts.

It can be intimidating to put yourself in front of a broad audience, but if you have a passion for something, it will show when you make posts and interact on social media. As long as you are staying true to yourself, others are going to take notice. The best part about doing your own advertising is that you get to control exactly how you'd like to portray yourself. It doesn't cost any money to make a few posts and gain notoriety. Over time, this just might be what your business needs in order to get a jump start.

Pros and Cons

Anyone can succeed in the business of social media marketing. All it takes is access to the internet and the willingness to interact with your followers. You need to be on top of current trends, and you must be tech-savvy. Growing a brand or advertising an existing one by way of social media is the perfect start to making a side income for the first time.

Pros:

- Work From Anywhere: You don't have to leave your home to make a post on social media. Interaction with your followers is fun and easy to do, and it can be done virtually anywhere you are. Because you don't have a rigid schedule to follow, social media marketing is even appropriate for those who already have a grueling full-time job. Whenever you have a few minutes to spare, you can get onto your accounts.
- Be Your Own Boss: The amount of work that you put into your social media marketing is up to your own discretion. If you want to go the extra mile and reach out to several brands daily, then you can. If you would rather grow your accounts organically and see what comes to you, you can also do that. The amount of time and effort you put into it is totally up to you.
- It Is an Ever-Growing Industry: Social media is a huge part of life in 2019. Almost everyone uses it, and it continues to grow rapidly. Becoming a part of something that is already thriving is a great business practice.
- There Is a Niche for Everything: No matter what you are interested in, there is likely already a niche that has been developed and a community of active users with an interest in it. Most of the guesswork has already been taken care of for you with social media marketing.
- You Will Enjoy It: Most jobs are stressful and fast-paced, but social media is something that you can do on your own time. It is likely that you already enjoy using social media daily, so why not turn it into something that can earn you an extra income?

Cons:

- You Need Patience: If you want to see instant growth, you will probably end up disappointed. While some people get lucky and get noticed right away, it is a rarity. It can take some time to build up your following and reputation, but as long as you are willing to put in the effort, you will start to see the growth.

- Be Aware of Scams: While a lot of brands out there truly do want your representation, some are looking to swindle you out of money. Be careful who you choose to work with, and just like any other business transaction, always read anything that they might ask you to sign. A simple observation of their profile is a good indication of a brand's validity. If you notice that their follower count is high, yet their interactions are computer-generated, steer clear.

- Luck is Involved: Hard work will get you places in any industry, but being an influencer does have an element of luck to it. You might be posting quality, consistent content, only to be overshadowed by someone else who is doing the same thing. This is why it is super important to solidify your niche and set yourself apart from the rest.

- Trends Change: Just as quickly as something rises to popularity on the internet, something else will come along and take its place. Because the web is ever-changing, you might notice that your followers will tire of your posts after some time. Be sure to leave room in your personal brand for transformation, just in case you see a decline in your niche.

- Beware of Fake Followers: Some people take advantage of the system by purchasing fake followers. While this does not earn them interaction, it boosts their numbers and makes them appear more appealing to work with. Companies cannot determine how or when you got your followers, but they do see the current number. This is an unfair advantage for those who work on getting followers organically.

Shopify Dropshipping

If you are unfamiliar with the company, Shopify is a platform that is designed to help you manage your own business. It is your one-stop shop for customization of an online portal for the products that you would like to sell. People use it for a variety of reasons, from selling clothing to art. It is cloud-based and easy for all to use. Many enjoy the perks that it comes with because the ability to list, manage, and sell inventory all in one place is highly efficient. Shopify gives you the opportunity to get noticed not only on social media, but on other online marketplaces and even physical shops as well.

Dropshipping: The Business Model

Because this guide is designed to teach you about ways you can make money online, focusing on Shopify dropshipping is going to be the smartest business tactic you can make. Operating your own business can take a lot of work, but with the dropshipping model, one of the most time-consuming steps is eliminated. Dropshipping follows a simple model -- the customer visits your ecommerce store and purchases a product at a retail price, you are paid a percentage of the wholesale price while paying the supplier the rest, and then the supplier sends the customer the goods directly.

Without having to worry about doing the shipping yourself, you will be free to further customize and streamline your ecommerce store. A lot of businesses, big and small, are turning to dropshipping for their business needs. If you are looking for a quick way to make extra money, this method can become very successful for you. Without having to be concerned with physically storing your inventory, you will have much more freedom than running your own traditional ecommerce store.

One of the most expensive parts of maintaining your own store is buying a surplus of inventory up front so that you have it in stock for your clients. This is where dropshipping can save you money -- You won't have to buy any inventory until you have officially made a sale. As you can see, even those with a very minimal budget can start an ecommerce store using the dropshipping business model.

Aside from not being responsible for inventory, you also don't have to worry about packing and shipping the products. This is a huge time saver for someone who is looking to use

Shopify as a side income platform. Even if you already have a full-time job, or just have limited free time due to school, you can successfully run your own ecommerce business using the dropshipping business model.

Realistically, as long as you have steady internet access, you can run your business from your phone or laptop for less than $100 each month. As long as you are able to stay on top of communications with your clients and suppliers, you can even run your business on the go. With the help of your supplier, you won't have to worry about the business growing beyond your means. No matter how much it grows, as long as you are putting the orders in, they will take care of the rest.

Despite all of the convenience and flexibility, you must remember that this is still a business that you are responsible for. You will need to frequently check your emails and make sure that everything is running smoothly. While you are not alone in the endeavor, it is still your own business that you will be held accountable for.

How to Get Started

The first step is to create a Shopify account. This is your chance to create your username and business name. Even if you are unsure about what you would like to call your business, don't worry about it! You can change the name in the future. You could go from selling sports memorabilia to opening your own clothing boutique. The flexibility is an excellent feature. Creating an account is free for the first 14 days. They give everybody this free trial to see if owning an ecommerce business is the right fit for them. After this, a basic plan costs around $29 per month and can increase accordingly depending on if you would like to select a more advanced plan.

After your account has been created, Shopify will ask you what brings you to the site. You can select options such as "I'm selling, just not online" or "I'm not selling products yet." Alternatively, you can even select "I'm just playing around," if you still are unsure about committing to running a business. Once you determine your reason for being on the site, then you will be redirected to your store dashboard. From here, you can control your listings and your themes. There is also a chance for you to set up your own custom domain.

The theme that comes with your store for free is the Shopify basic theme. There are plenty of other free themes that you can utilize. As you get more serious about your store, you can purchase a theme or hire someone to create a theme for you. Within each theme, you will be provided with customization options. This is where you can design your header and footer; you can also add photos to each section. Again, nothing is set in stone. If you design your theme to your liking, you can change it in the future when you think of new ideas.

Choosing your domain is a way you can help your customers remember your shop; it is a customized website name. If you select one on Shopify, your website URL will look something like this: www.xyz.myshopify.com -- While this isn't the worst format, it can seem a little bit long. But as a starting point, it is great and it is free. If you become more serious about your store, you can purchase a custom domain name that will change your website name to something a lot more simplified: www.xyz.com. Again, purchasing a domain isn't a requirement, but it could become helpful in the future.

The Oberlo App

Once you have all of the details of your account set up with Shopify, you will need to download an app called Oberlo. This app is designed by Shopify to work with their system. It is your place to connect with suppliers and to decide what kind of products that you would like to sell to your clients. Through a "Products" menu, you will be able to search through thousands of items. If you decide that you would like to sell several different products, this is possible through the Oberlo app.

Once you begin selecting products, you can link them straight to your Shopify store. The app also gives you suggestions and ideas for boosting your sales. They show you items that are normally sold together in stores, and allow you the option to add them into your own store. This can be the most time consuming, but most fun, part of the process. Deciding where you would like to take your brand is a very important part of operating an ecommerce store.

For example, a store that is called Picasso Plus might specialize in selling Picasso-themed items. This can include, pens, mugs, shirts, and more that display his artwork on each item. It might take some brainstorming for you to fully decide which direction you'd like to take with your store. Make sure that you are certain of your target audience, and then think about the kind of products that would be most appealing to that group. It is also wise to consider what you would find interesting. Think about what kind of products you would like to be included to buy online.

Using Oberlo not only provides you an organized way to stock your shop, but it also allows you the peace of mind to know that you are going to be working with verified suppliers. The app pre-screens each supplier to ensure that they meet the standards that are put in place by Shopify. Doing this on your own would pose too much of a risk, as you do not have the same tools at your disposal for the screening process.

Keep in mind that, during your supplier search, you will likely have to decide if you want your supplier to be located in the US or if you are okay with one that is based in China (or elsewhere). Including "ePacket" items means that you would like to give your clients the option to purchase these foreign-based products for low shipping costs. If you do not wish to do this, you can exclude this option when you are searching for products to stock your shop with. Naturally, US-based items are going to ship faster, but excluding ePacket items will narrow down your potential inventory options.

During your search for products, you can filter the results by price points. If you have a specific vision for your shop, you can determine the minimum or maximum amount that you would like to sell an item for. When you are performing these product searches, you will be given a rating for each item. This will help you to decide if you'd like to list said item in your own store. Oberlo has plenty of resources to assist you as you build your store.

Stocking your shop is as simple as clicking a button. As mentioned, the products that you select on Oberlo get linked directly to your Shopify account. Keep in mind the following as you are stocking your store:

- Make sure that you are writing accurate product descriptions. Oberlo provides you with the basic details that you need, but modifying each one is a way to make the connection that you have with your clients more personal.
- Choose what you think is a fair price. Oberlo sets a default price for you, but you have the option to modify this. Do some research on your own, and see what other sellers are offering for the same or similar products. Your shop won't succeed if you are selling an item that appears very overpriced in relation to other shops.
- Because the shipping time is not up to you, disclose to your customers what their

estimated wait time is. It is best to be very transparent about this in order to keep your customers happy.

- In the beginning, it is recommended that you select about 10-20 products to start with. This will give your store enough variety, but will also keep it looking organized and maintained. As you see how your clients respond to the given items, you can then modify your stock. You can either swap or add items as you see fit. This is the best way to run your shop when you are just starting out on Shopify. By doing this, you won't be wasting time on writing a ton of product descriptions for products that might not even be desired by your client base.

It is all a matter of trial and error when it comes to running your own business. While it can be hard to just wait and see, this is what normally needs to be done. Oberlo will show you what your statistics are, and from there, you will be able to see which items are most in demand. When you do decide to expand your inventory, try going based on the trends that you see, either in your statistics, or in other shops that are similar.

Once you have your list of products linked over to your Shopify account, you can go in and create different categories or "collections" for the items. This will be a way for you to organize everything and make sure that your clients have an efficient shopping experience. With this, you just have to use your common sense to determine which items should be placed together. This is another great opportunity to imagine yourself in your clients' shoes. What would you expect to see in terms of categorization?

Maintaining Your Shop

Much like a shop with a physical location, you are going to want to monitor customer activity as your business develops. Remember that Oberlo will be able to give you some insight into this. If you notice that your customers are responding well to mugs in the first month, consider expanding your selection. The Shopify App Store is a place where you can search for additional places to source your products. The following are some examples:

- POD Shippers: POD stands for print-on-demand. A POD shipper will allow you access to a range of fully customizable products. This is where you can let your creative side flourish -- designing the looks of your products via these third party apps will give your shop a unique edge.

- Specialty Shippers: This type of shipper is normally meant for products that you cannot get in your home country. Some people use specialty shippers to sell their clients goods, such as coffee. This can be a cool element to introduce to your Shopify customers.
- Aggregate Shippers: For larger quantities of items, some that are even name brand items, you are going to want to look into an aggregate shipper. Sometimes, if your shop gains traction quickly, it is smart to switch over to one of these larger shipping companies.

Aside from making sure that your shop is fully prepared to handle its orders, you are also going to need to do some customer outreach. Being more personable toward your clients will make them feel valued. There are a couple of different ways to make sure that you are communicating effectively with your clients. The first way is by creating and utilizing social media pages for your business. Not only does this give you multiple platforms to advertise on, but it also gives your clients a way to easily contact you and give you feedback on your shop.

Another way to stay in touch with clients is by having them sign up for marketing emails that you create. Shopify has ways to do this that are already built in and ready to be accessed by each shop owner. Remember, this about the content that you would like to receive from a retail store. There is no need to spam your clients with information that is too repetitive or not relevant. Stay short and concise -- a lot of successful shops offer discount coupons within their newsletters in order to entice customers to join the mailing list.

Consider your use of SEO keywords. Even in your short product descriptions, you should be thinking about the way that you are utilizing certain keywords. If your shop is SEO formatted, you will be appearing higher in the search engine results. If you are unsure of how to format your shop with the correct keywords, you can take a look at some of Shopify's built-in tools that are designed to help.

Things to Remember

The role of the dropshipper is an invisible one. The customer sees your store as the interface, and goes off of what they see there to determine if they would like to make a purchase. You are the direct link between your customers and the products that they receive, even if you are not the one who is doing the packing and shipping. This is why communication is so essential as a shop owner. For any order-related inquiries, your customers are going to be counting on you to keep them in the loop.

You are also responsible for relaying any messages from the shipper to the customer. If you know that the shipper is located in China and requires a 2-3 week ship time, then it would be morally incorrect to tell your customers that they can expect their products in 1 week. Simple business practices like this one will set you apart from being a scam type of shop to a successful one that customers can trust. Word of mouth can be a great free source of advertisement. If you make a good impression on one person, they might go ahead and tell five of their friends.

Presentation of your products matters, too. If a customer were to click onto your shop, and all of the items were disorganized and hard to find, it is unlikely that they are going to make a purchase. You have to remember, much like any other traditional business, you have competition. If a customer does not find your shop streamlined and appealing, there are plenty of other places on Shopify (and elsewhere online) where they can spend their money. The more effort you put into your presentation, the more it will be recognized.

When you first start out on Shopify, you will probably have to make a checklist to ensure that you are doing everything correctly. Hold onto this list, and keep referring back to it as your shop develops. Even if you are not just starting from scratch, some of the information could be a valuable reminder to yourself. Owning your own business does require a lot of hard work and effort. Just because you do not have to physically show up to a workplace does not mean that it will automatically be a breeze. You will need to wear many different hats and utilize several of your skills, from designing the theme of your shop to providing excellent customer service.

Some of the items on your checklist can include the following:

- Get Your Domain Secured: Even if you start out with one of the domain options that are available through Shopify, you will probably need to think of some domain name ideas for the future. Having your own customized domain gives your shop a professional look, and it makes it easier for your customers to remember your shop.

- Secure Your Payment Portal: In order to get paid for your sales, you will need to make sure that your customers' payments are going to go through. The easiest way to do this is by making a test sale using your own card information. Once you make sure that everything works, you can refund yourself so that no money is lost.

- Make Sure Landing Pages Are Completed: When you launch your shop, you should make sure that all pages that your customers have access to are finished. This involves everything from selecting a theme, writing content, and adding images. Aside from a standard home page, some other popular landing pages are "About" and "Contact." Both are important for different reasons -- The "About" page explains your shop mission, while the "Contact" page lets customers know how they can get in touch with you.

- Review Your Email Settings: Through Shopify, you have access to several email templates that send out automatically. This is a great tool to utilize, because it makes client outreach effortless. You can go into these templates and create your own edits, making sure that you are sending the right message to your clients.

- Audit Your Content: Running your own store can be a lot of work, so it is wise to get an outside opinion. Have a friend or family member view your store, and allow them to provide honest input. This is also a great time for catching small spelling errors or possible broken links.

- Streamline the Images You Choose: If your site loads its images at different speeds, this could be because they are different sizes. Try to resize your images to the same or similar size. This not only promotes cohesiveness, but it also lends a more streamlined look to your shop. Also, try to select images that go well together. This could mean anything from having a similar theme to having the same color scheme. Your shop will appear more professional if the images make sense together.

- Install Analytics: While Shopify provides you with their own sets of analytics tools, it might be wise to also set up a third-party tool to keep track of your site visitors. You will be able to see where your customers come from, what time they visit, and how long they spend on each page. This information can come in handy when you are trying to decide how to market your products.

Pros and Cons

Utilizing Shopify for dropshipping is becoming increasingly popular. Because of the wide variety of products that can be kept in stock, many people find it is a great way to quickly start up a business. The tools that Shopify has to offer truly makes the process simple and accessible for all, no complicated software included.

Pros:

- You Can Sell Nearly Anything: No matter what kind of shop you open, you have a wide array of products to choose from. Whether you want to specialize in customized mugs, or if you want to stock an entire clothing store, Shopify gives you the platform to grow on.
- Your Shop Can Be Broad or Niche: The freedom to customize your shop at any time is great for your own personal branding. Whether you want to create a specialty shop, or one that appeals to the masses, anything is possible.
- No Physical Commitment: You are never required to be anywhere at any given time. This is what makes Shopify dropshipping a great option for making quick money online. The products essentially sell themselves, and you only need to monitor this in the background. There are no in-person meetings or interactions to worry about.
- It Can Be Easily Expanded: If your shop shows a promising amount of growth, keeping it stocked up is as easy as pressing a button. Since you do not need to worry about purchasing huge amounts of your inventory in bulk, you will easily be able to accommodate your customers if they begin to multiply.
- It Pays for Itself: Once your Shopify free trial is up, you must pay a monthly fee to keep your shop running. The business will very easily begin to pay for itself within the first few sales that you make. This type of turnaround in a business is very rare, but the Shopify platform makes it almost effortless.

Cons:

- It Is an Investment: Yes, owning a store on Shopify costs money. With that membership, though, you are a platform with plenty of different tools that will help you out along the way. If you are not prepared for this monthly commitment, then owning your own business is probably not the best step for you to take in order to make additional income. You might also have to deal with a slight overlap in getting paid and ordering the customer's product. It is wise to prepare for any type of possibility.

- You Might Not Gain Traction Quickly: While there is a chance to greatly succeed on Shopify, it is important to remember the risk involved -- you are going to have to rely on a bit of luck. Building up your reputation with your customers can take time, so remember that as you are first starting out. Your success probably won't happen overnight, but if you stay committed to working on your shop, you should start seeing tangible results.

- There is Competition: There is a high chance that you will have direct competition on Shopify. This is okay! Use this as motivation to do better. Think about all of the different places that you can choose to buy a mug. What are some of the factors that help you narrow down where you would like to buy a mug from? Thinking about things from the customer's perspective will help you a lot when it comes to the way that you operate your shop.

- You Aren't in Control: When you sell a product to a customer, you are then relying on your shipper to do the rest. This can be both a relief and a burden, at times. Because it is out of your hands, you need to be prepared to take the brunt of the situation when shipping takes longer than expected or when a customer has a missing item in their package. Steady communication between yourself, your customers, and your shipper is essential for running a successful business.

- Expect Low Profits to Start: Your business will need to grow gradually, so you can expect your profits to the do the same. You are getting a percentage of the profits when you decide to partner with a drop shipper. Many people are discouraged by this, but you will likely be thankful in the future when your shop is bigger and you do not have to worry about packing and shipping.

Airbnb Agency

Airbnb has become a huge industry in several cities all around the world. It is often a cheaper and better way to explore a city that you are visiting, all without the need to stay in a single hotel room for the duration of your trip. Being a part of an Airbnb agency does not involve renting out your own living space. Instead, you are helping others rent out *their* homes. An Airbnb agency is designed to help the property owner and the renter connect. Sometimes, these agencies even offer services such as setting optimal pricing for the home, restocking items in the home, and cleaning the home. Of course, if you are looking to make an online side income, you would only need to be a part of the services that would suit your own schedule.

You can start your own agency, and you can even have others working for you, all from the comfort of your own home. In order to manage an Airbnb agency, you need to have excellent communication skills; this is going to make or break the business. While you do not physically need to meet with renters, you will want to make sure that you can stay on top of your emails and notifications. The main role of an Airbnb agency is to bridge the gap between the property owner and the renter. In case anyone needs help or has questions, you must be available to assist.

As you can imagine, you will need to have an extensive understanding of Airbnb and the process of renting. This is not very hard to learn, especially if you have ever rented a space on Airbnb yourself. There are several tutorials and videos online that go into all of the details that you will need; it just takes a little bit of well-thought-out research. Once you are knowledgeable enough on the industry, you will need to make a decision: Do you want to team up with an existing Airbnb agency or do you want to start your own?

Depending on how much time and money you have to start with, it might be easier to go with an existing agency in the beginning so that you can get a feel for the business. Either way, you are going to want to make sure that the agency explains its services very clearly. Some strictly offer booking/listing services, and you are going to want to make sure that your customers understand what you have to offer.

Getting Clients

In order to get Airbnb owners to work with you, the way you present yourself is very important. Like it has been mentioned, having personal experience with Airbnb (either as a renter or an owner) is a big plus. Your clients are going to trust you more if they trust that you have an understanding of the industry. Gaining this trust is essential, because without property owners that are willing to work with you, there would be no need for an Airbnb agency. The trick is to convince the owner that they would be better off using your services than listing their property on their own.

Explain the services that are being offered in a clear and concise way. You will not want to imply that the agency will clean the home and provide key exchanges, when the only services offered are booking/listing and vice versa. Credibility is everything when it comes to this type of business. You should not have to offer your clients any gimmicks in order for them to be willing to work with you; it should be very black and white when it comes to what you have to offer. Once you have secured the client base, the business should flourish naturally.

Essentially, these properties are being put into your hands, so you must prove to your clients that you are able to deliver your promise. Tell them why they should work with you, and be honest about what you have to offer. This is the best way to succeed in an industry involving home rentals. A good approach is to mention that other property management companies can be too big and overpriced. Many consist of several different employees and ask for too much of a percentage of the profit. Being a part of a smaller agency will allow the customer to talk to the same person (or few people) each time. This personal connection builds trust in an easy way. Simply knowing who they can turn to with questions and concerns will give you a higher chance of gaining their business.

Why Airbnb Agencies Are Important

One of the main reasons a person might want to use an Airbnb agency is to avoid being scammed. Unfortunately, there are many people (property owners and renters alike) who do try to scam others for money. Renting an Airbnb through an agency is a way to ensure that you are making a smart, pre-screened selection. Also, a lot of property owners are merely renters themselves. This means that someone who is renting an apartment might be listing their apartment on Airbnb for a brief time while they are elsewhere. This isn't always a scam, because some landlords are okay with subletting. But, it can be illegal, and a lease violation in some places. If you are renting someone's apartment without landlord permission, you might be in for an ugly surprise if the landlord finds out.

Another reason a property owner might want to seek out an agency to work with is because they simply don't want to deal with the follow-up that comes with Airbnb. If the property owner is also on the go, it might be inconvenient for them to have to keep up with communications from potential renters. It can often be an overwhelming process, so taking on the help of a third party to bridge this gap makes sense.

It is the intention of an Airbnb agency to make sure that everything that is going on is safe and legal. Both the property owner and renter will be thankful to have that middleman to monitor such activities. In order to do this, you must be efficient with time and organization. Attention to detail is a must. You won't want to accidentally double-book a property or forget to pay a client. While being a part of an Airbnb agency is a more involved way to make money online, it can become a very successful side business for you to rely on.

From the start, you should have a system in place that you can follow. These standard procedures should cover your bases, and can be referenced along the way in case you encounter any issues. For example, there should be a plan in place both before you begin operating and during your operations. Some things to consider are the following:

- Think about whether you would like to join an existing agency, or start your own. Both are realistic ways for you to make money on the side, but naturally, starting your own Airbnb agency is likely going to be more time consuming because of the extra steps that you will need to take.

- Decide which services you will provide. As mentioned, some Airbnb agencies are full service. They start by booking/listing Airbnbs, and they continue to assist with everything from the key exchange to the restocking of the home. No matter how extensive you would like to get, just make sure that you know what you are getting yourself into from the start.

- Make sure that you are all caught up on the basic rules and regulations that surround the Airbnb industry. Knowledge is everything when it comes to being a part of a successful business. You need to be able to confidently answer any questions that come your way.

- Once you are ready to start working, come up with a basic outline of what you need to do each day in order to keep the agency running smoothly. This can be anything from answering emails, to ensuring that all listings are properly uploaded.
- Decide on your niche. Sometimes, it can be helpful to differentiate yourself from other businesses; this will give you less competition. Instead of only listing regular apartments/homes through your agency, maybe you could only focus on properties that are beachfront. This is a way that you can set yourself apart from the crowd. Anything can become your niche, and some brainstorming might be required.
- Consider how you are going to handle payment exchanges. You are going to need a valid and safe system in place if you want to get paid. Selecting a payment portal will also take a certain amount of research on your end, but there are a wide variety to choose from available online.
- Become familiar with the properties. When your clients come to you with their properties that they would like you to list, take the time to actually look into what they have to offer. How many bedrooms are available? Is it a shared space, or is it a private space? It will show your dedication if you are able to provide a detailed listing versus some generic write-up of your clients' properties. Remember, you are trying to make these properties as appealing as you can to the potential renters.
- Don't be afraid to hustle! A big component of an Airbnb agency is getting your client a decent price on their listing, and this can involve some negotiation. If you know that your client is expecting an unreasonable amount of money for their rental, you need to be able to provide them with valid alternative suggestions. Be diplomatic, yet honest, and explain how you came to your conclusions on price points. This can take a little bit of practice on your end, and becoming familiar with other listings on Airbnb is a great way to get this experience. Look for listings that have similar features, or are in similar areas. This is the best way to choose a smart, yet fair, price point.

Think Outside the Box

Remember that there are several different ways to run the same business. If you would like to start your own Airbnb agency, you can specialize in different niches, as it was mentioned before. Plenty of people like to stay by the beach when they are on vacation. If you live in an area that has access to water, using the beach as a niche is a quick way to gain traction and appeal. It is an automatic selling point, and it will keep many different people interested in the properties that you have to offer. If you are located in an area with forests, you can try to seek clients that are looking to rent out their cabins to others. Renting a cabin in the woods is a classic vacation that plenty of people take, and it might even be more feasible for people to rent an Airbnb instead of going through expensive cabin rental agencies.

Another niche that you can use is large spaces. Often, people will decide to rent an Airbnb over a hotel room because they have a lot of people that would like to all stay together. This is possible in an Airbnb, especially in larger homes. If you have plenty of space to offer your clients, this will solve the need for renting multiple different units. You might also get recurring customers, because they will know that you have the rentals that can accommodate all of the people in their party. Alternatively, people rent out their small apartments on Airbnb, and someone who is traveling alone might see this as the best option. Instead of paying for a hotel room with all of the amenities included, spending half that price on an Airbnb apartment might make more sense.

Airbnbs that are pet-friendly can also become a niche for you to utilize. Not every hotel or motel accepts pets, and if they do, it is often for a sizeable additional fee each night. Some people who rent out their homes are perfectly okay with guests bringing along their furry friends. Use this to your advantage, and make it a selling point. A lot of people like to travel with their pets, so they are going to need special accommodations. The great part about Airbnb is that you will find a wide variety of spaces that are available for rent, so using pet-friendly locations as a niche can become something that you are well known for.

Once you are settled on a niche, you can use other perks to your advantage. Express to your clients that, by using an Airbnb agency, they are going to be able to spend more time enjoying the vacation and less time worrying about the planning. You will need to allow them to see that you are there to help, and that your service is meant to make the planning easier. The same goes for the property owners: You need to show them that using an Airbnb agency is more helpful than trying to list their own properties.

In order to accomplish this, you must have great people skills. No matter if you choose to run your own agency, or become a part of an existing one, you will be communicating with people frequently. This job can definitely be a side hustle in addition to a regular full-time job, but the more effort you put into it, the more success you will begin to see. As long as you are able to spend a little bit of time on it each day, then you should have no problem keeping up with your clients' needs.

People are going to want your opinion on different marketing strategies. This is another main reason why someone would want to list their property via an agency. Expressing your opinions and providing advice is also going to become a part of your daily task list. You don't need to have a degree in marketing, but you do need to make sure that you are up-to-speed on the current most successful marketing techniques in order to help your clients. It is okay to think outside of the box; be honest with your clients, and bounce some ideas off of them to determine what would be the best way to list their properties.

You can mention the different niches that you have thought of, and various other selling points. Basically, anything that adds value to the property, whether it is merely for looks or serves a greater purpose, can be used as a positive selling point. See what your client has to say about the space, and you will probably think of even more ways that you can market the property.

Pro tip: Advertising properties as "the only" gives them an extra air of exclusivity, and thus, allows you to charge higher prices.

E.g. "The only 3 bedroom beachfront property on this street", "The only Georgian townhouse on the Upper East side with an elevator for wheelchair users." You might not think a particular property is unique, but if you think outside the box, you'll be sure to come up with something.

Coming Up With a Price

Arguably the most difficult job when working with real estate, you must come up with a fair price point to list each Airbnb. Not only do you have to set a price that is fair to the property owner, but you must also set one that will appeal to the potential renters. It might be difficult to simply take a look at a property and then decide on a number on the spot. You can use a few of these techniques for determining your price points:

- Get an idea of what other similar properties are being rented for. You wouldn't want to list a 2-bedroom home for $200 a night when similar homes were being rented for only $100. To compare these figures, you might just need to get on Airbnb and do a little bit of filtered searching on your own.

- Once you have seen what similar properties are being rented for, do a broader search of the city or town. It is unlikely that someone is going to come into town and rent the only expensive property while the rest remain in a lower price bracket. It takes a simple search and some common sense to ensure that you are within the means of the price bracket.

- Have a conversation with your client before the listing goes up. In addition to what you would like to say about the property when you list it, you will be discussing the pricing with your client. Whenever you present them with numbers, make sure that you have credible reasoning for why you have chosen them. Example: "I think that you should rent your home for $80 a night, because similar homes in the areas are seeing success at this price point." It is all about incentive when you are trying to make a sale.

- Don't forget the time of year that the client is trying to rent out their property. If it is a holiday season, it might be more valid to charge a little bit more money for the rental because of the higher demand. You wouldn't necessarily want to list a place for the same amount in June as you would during Christmas. Take a look at the calendar on Airbnb when you are doing your comparative searches.

- If your client is new to renting, it would be worthwhile to suggest that they try to keep their pricing down in order to be competitive. Without an established reputation in place, having a lower price is a major selling point. Especially because the AirBNB platform relies so heavily on user ratings. As renters begin to give the property ratings, this will boost its popularity and place it in higher demand. After this, you might be able to suggest raising the price.

Pros and Cons

Working in an industry that deals with accommodation is a sure way to stay relevant. When travel is involved, visitors are going to need a place to stay. Working as an Airbnb agent also provides you with the chance to help people. Not only is it an important job, but it can also become meaningful. You will get to interact with a variety of people and learn about various properties.

Pros:

- It Can Become a Lucrative Career: Doing work in real estate always has the potential for growth. You might find that you enjoy it enough to take things to the next level. While being a part of an Airbnb agency can start out as an online side hustle, it can just as easily transform into your full-time business.
- The Industry Will Always Be in Demand: People are always going to need places to stay when they travel. Unlike other industries, you will always find a market for those seeking vacation rentals. This is a great factor in deciding whether or not you would like to become a part of the industry. No matter when you join, there will always be plenty of demand.
- You Will Learn a Lot About Your Area: By listing various properties all over your city, you might discover new places that you have never seen before. This can come in handy for when you would like to rent your own vacation home, or even if you are looking to move your permanent residence. By default, you will be more familiar with the area that you reside in, because you are often going to be comparing similar properties.
- You Get to Help People: By connecting renters to property owners, you are bridging a gap and allowing the business transaction to operate smoothly. If you enjoy working directly with people, you will likely find interest in working for an Airbnb agency. This can be a nice change of pace if your day job does not involve much outside interaction. You will have the ability to let your personality shine through and to get to know others.
- Use of Creativity is Encouraged: Appeal is what you are striving for when you are listing properties for rent. Your client is going to be counting on you to get them the

best rate for their rental. Alternatively, renters are going to be searching for the best place to stay during their vacations. This is when you can allow your creativity to flourish. You will be able to use photos, descriptive keywords, and niches in order to convince renters why they should choose the given property as their rental. You can have a lot of fun with this part, coming up with ways that you think might appeal to the masses.

Cons:

- It Can Become Time Consuming: While being a part of an Airbnb agency qualifies as a side hustle, it might become a lot to handle for a single person. If you are already working a full-time job and you are trying to list properties during a busy holiday season, you might find yourself overwhelmed with the amount of work that you are responsible for.

- It Is a Commitment: Because you are not putting your own property up for rent, you do not get to just decide that you don't want to put in the work any longer when you get tired of it. The property owner will be counting on you to fulfill a commitment, so you probably don't want to get on board with a job like this if you are not in it for the long haul. You need to make sure that every aspect of the rental goes smoothly, from the listing to the check out.

- Seasons Impact Growth: As previously touched upon, the need for a vacation rental during a holiday season is much higher than during any other average time. While there is always a fairly steady stream of demand, you might not see the most growth during the seasons that are not peak seasons. If you are looking for fast money, you might want to consider working in the industry during some of the most high-demand times (Christmas, Thanksgiving, New Year's Eve, etc...).

- Conflict Can Arise: When you are working with any number of people, it can be easy to clash. You will need to make sure that the rental process goes smoothly for the property owner and the renter, so if you are not up for the role of mediator, then you might want to reconsider working for an Airbnb agency.

- You Might Get in Over Your Head: If you are just starting out in the industry, it might feel a bit overwhelming. In order to prevent any unnecessary stress, you should start out with an Airbnb agency that is already well established. Having a team of people to help you out with your workload will likely be better than trying to take on all of the tasks by yourself from the start. After you have the experience under your belt, you will likely be more successful if you decide that you want to start your own agency.

Amazon FBA

FBA stands for "Fulfillment By Amazon," and it is becoming a fast-growing way for you to make extra money. This service is very similar to a dropshipping service; you are able to sell a wide variety of products through your own store on Amazon. Once you have your inventory scheduled, you will then send it off to an Amazon warehouse in bulk, and then they will take care of the rest. Once sales are made, the warehouse will ship the items to each individual client. This streamlined way of running a store is the best way to operate your own business when you are looking to make some extra income on the side.

The Amazon Marketplace is an ecommerce marketplace owned by Amazon that will host your store. Because of this, you will have exposure to anyone who chooses to browse Amazon for products. As you can imagine, the amount of people that shop on Amazon each day is exponentially growing. One difference between a regular dropshipper and this one is that you can sell products that are both new and used. If you have some items that you are no longer using, you can list them on your store to earn some quick money. It's like a virtual garage sale. There is a real opportunity for success if you decide that you'd like to sell products by using Amazon FBA.

How to Get Started

The first step to selling on Amazon is to make a Selling on Amazon account. From there, you can then add FBA as one of the features on your account. These first few steps are simple and should only take you a couple of minutes to complete. Before you begin, you might need to consider what you'd like your business email address to be, because you should sign up for your account with that designated email. If you are only going to be selling a couple of your own items and you do not wish to create a business email, then your personal one will work just fine.

Once your account is set up, you can begin listing your inventory. You can start to add products to your catalogue one at a time or in bulk. If you are experienced and have inventory management software in place already, you should be able to just upload your existing inventory directly onto Amazon. The same thought process goes into FBA as it would with any other dropshipping business. You will need to figure out what you would like to sell.

Start by considering if you would like to stock your shop with items that are already listed in the catalogue, or if you would like to sell your own items. Depending on which direction you decide to go in, your next action can vary. If you are selling your own used items, you will need to take a little bit of extra time coming up with the proper photos and descriptions for each one. If you are going to be selling handmade goods, this will also require extra time for obvious reasons.

The easiest way to begin on FBA when you are looking to make quick money is to stock your shop with products that are already listed on Amazon. This method does not require any additional work on your end to gather/supply the products. If you need shipping supplies, Amazon has you covered. You are able to buy product prep supplies directly from the source, and they have plenty of Amazon-preferred packaging to help you easily get your items to their warehouse.

There are several tools to assist you during this process. Amazon partners with carriers that offer discounted shipping rates. This way, you will be able to keep your inventory stocked without breaking the bank. These discounts are available if you are looking to ship small/individual parcels or items that are shipped on pallets (either less than a truckload or an entire truckload). With these parameters, you will likely qualify for the discounts that are available.

Aside from the discounted rate, these partner carriers also supply things such as shipping labels. All you will need to do is order all of your items, pack them up, and place the predetermined label on the box. Keep in mind that if you are going to be shipping truckloads of items, you will need to have a dock and forklift. This type of service is for shops that are bigger and well-established. When you are first starting out, you will likely only be sending a few boxes at a time to the warehouse.

Benefits to Using FBA

Once everything is fully stocked, you will be ready to make some sales. This is when you will see the return on your investments. A great thing about partnering with Amazon is that your customers will receive the same customer service that any traditional Amazon customer would. The interface looks exactly the same, and any questions that arise will be sent over to Amazon to be dealt with. This takes a lot of pressure off of you as a seller, because you don't have to be the one to answer to your customers' inquiries or concerns. As you can see, this is another way that FBA differs from traditional dropshipping systems.

For anyone trying to make a side income online, it is important that the business provides as much convenience as possible. With FBA, these needs will be met. You do not have to worry about physically storing any of the inventory at your home. All you must be responsible for is the ordering and bulk shipping to the warehouse. They provide your items with a space to stay until a sale is made. With this type of system, it is possible for anyone to open a successful ecommerce store. A lot of people are seeing fast results that generate additional income.

Because your shop is being "hosted" by Amazon, your products will pop up on their search results. There are millions of searches daily for just about anything that you can think of. Amazon does their best to boost the product listings of those being sold by FBA users. This means, if someone is looking to buy bandages, Amazon will try to boost your search result over a larger name-brand company. It is a way to receive built-in advertisement that is provided to you because you have decided to partner with Amazon.

Your item can also qualify for Prime shipping, Amazon's expedited shipping service. This is a huge perk to those customers who are looking to get their items quickly. As long as they have a Prime membership in place, they will be able to select Prime shipping on any of the items that you are selling. This is another form of built-in advertisement. A lot of times, customers put on search filters to only show Prime-ready items.

Because Amazon has been around for such a long time, and is a well-established business already, you can have the confidence to know that your customers will be taken care of. Even if you are brand new to ecommerce, you are covered under an umbrella that has a team of people ready to help you and your customers. This is a much easier way for you to start a shop rather than attempting to sell your items organically. The Amazon platform already exists, and the opportunity is as big as you would like to make it.

Fees and Pricing

Using FBA is an investment, so if you are unwilling to put money into your business, then this is not the right business for you. The bottom line is that you will need to be willing to stock your shop with inventory before you can begin seeing a return profit. You will also need to consider the cost of shipping to the fulfillment warehouse. If you are unsure about this business model, you can start by shipping one single box of items to the warehouse for your inventory. When this runs out, then you can decide if you would like to continue running your own store.

With FBA, it can cost anywhere from $2-$5 to ship items to the warehouse. If you have oversized items, the price can be anywhere between $8-$150. There are shipping rates on Amazon that you can refer to when you are deciding what size box you will need to send. Even if you decide to send the smallest box of inventory to the warehouse, your customers will still have the same access -- they will be able to purchase products from your store, speak with customer service, and process refunds if need be.

There is a small storage fee that is required if you have inventory in the Amazon warehouse. The fee is deducted monthly, and it depends on the month of the year and the amount of average space that your items are taking up. Between January to September, the fee is $0.69 per cubic foot for a standard storage unit and $0.48 for an oversized unit. For October-December the pricing is $2.40/$1.20. This pricing goes up due to holiday demand, but keep in mind that you will likely also see an increase in sales during this time.

Amazon does provide you with a small price cut, as you can see, if you decide that you need an oversized storage unit. By selecting this unit, this means that you are likely more serious about your shop and plan to keep it regularly stocked with items. If you are still unsure about which plan that you will need to get started, opt for a standard unit. You can always change this in the future if you need more space.

If you are still on the fence about FBA, you can go online to use their price calculator. Not only will you be able to estimate your out of pocket fees, but you will also be able to see what your estimated profit will be. There are also a couple of product example charts for you to get an idea of how much space certain items require while in storage. For example, to store a 1-pound box of T-shirts, the average cost is around $3.68 per unit.

There is a special program in place called FBA Small and Light. This is for shops who know that they are not going to have a large amount of inventory, and it is great for first-timers who are still becoming familiar with the process. This service will help you by offering reduced fulfillment costs to certain items that can be ordered in smaller quantities. By keeping the costs down, your profit margins will naturally go up. This can be an excellent starting point for a beginner.

Another great thing is that there is no minimum purchase requirement when it comes to the Small and Light program. Your customers will receive the same great perks and service that they normally would. They still qualify for free shipping, and if they are Prime members, they will also qualify for the expedited Prime shipping option. If you think that this sounds like a good option to start with, take a look at the catalogue for qualified items.

An additional way that you can help your customers save money is by opting into Amazon's Subscribe and Save program. With the products that qualify, customers can agree to purchase your Subscribe and Save item, which will result in recurring deliveries of that item. It is a chance for your customers to conveniently get the items that they need, as well as you having a regular customer and sale. By obtaining customers through this program, it is also likely that they will return to your store and make more purchases.

Even despite your small investment, Amazon makes it easy for you to obtain business and keep it. They want you to succeed, because it is a mutually beneficial partnership. This is why using FBA will likely generate the success that you expect, instead of trying to open a store using only your own resources. Anyone can operate a FBA store, and any item(s) can be sold. The freedom to turn your store into exactly what you want is there, and the only thing you need is consistent initiative.

Helpful Programs

You should already be familiar with the different programs that Amazon has to offer, but here are some that you probably have never considered:

Permission to Sell Dangerous Goods -- It's good to have a niche, and in this case, you can have one that allows you to sell items that are normally not permitted to be sold via ecommerce websites. Through Amazon FBA, you are able to join a waitlist to get approval on selling these "dangerous" items. Some of which include: perfumes, household cleaners, paint, and certain beauty products. These items are in demand, but often hard to a first-time seller to obtain the rights to sell. Amazon gives you this opportunity if you wish to take it.

Sponsored Products -- Much like traditional social media marketing, you can also utilize sponsored posts to promote your items. There is a pay-per-click service available that allows you to put ads on Amazon. You only pay for the ad each time that it is clicked on, and you can set a maximum budget for your campaign. This is a great way to get noticed on the Amazon Marketplace.

Lightning Deals -- Amazon offers certain items at a discounted rate as a part of their Lightning Deals program. This is a limited sale of a certain item, and its exclusivity entices customer to make immediate purchases. If you would like to participate, you can set some of your items to be available as a deal in order to give your business a boost in sales.

Global Access -- You aren't limited to your local area when it comes to sales. If you wanted to, you could take your shop to the next level and sell globally. Obviously, this is quite the expansion of your client base. There are many different global programs that you can become a part of, from worldwide selling to targeted regions.

Handmade Items

The process for selling your own items is similar to selling pre-selected inventory. Of course, you will have to consider that the supply and demand levels are going to be much higher when you are creating the items that are for sale. If your shop becomes popular in a short amount of time, you will likely need to work extra to create enough inventory. Amazon has a community with creators from over 80 countries that sell their own handmade creations. If you would like to become a part of this niche, the application process is easy. Amazon still helps you with fulfillment, and you would send your creations to the warehouse the same way you would with any other inventory that you choose.

Amazon likes to screen all new applicants to ensure the quality of the items for sale. They don't want to mistakenly allow a seller a spot in the homemade marketplace when their items are actually just being purchased and resold. That is what the standard Amazon Marketplace is for. Once you meet the approval criteria, you are given several tools to utilize in your homemade shop. Just like any other shop, you have the opportunity to customize it to your liking. You can create a unique URL so that your customers will remember your shop easily.

Listing your handmade goods costs nothing. Everything from the process of joining Amazon Handmade to creating your shop is free. When you make a sale, Amazon will keep a 15%

referral fee, and that is the only catch! It is a worthwhile business move, especially if you truly do not have much to invest. When making your budget, all you will have to think about is the time and money that you are going to spend creating your products. Remember that these figures can increase by a lot if your shop gains traction.

If you aren't the most crafty person, you can still sell on Handmade if you like to customize ready-made items! For example, if you are good with a paint brush, you can paint custom mugs for people. Getting a large stock of basic mugs and some paint and brushes likely won't cost very much money, and it will be perfect to get you started. Your creativity can be unlimited on Amazon Handmade.

As was mentioned before, the same features of traditional Amazon FBA apply -- Once an order is placed, Amazon will pack and ship the item to your customer. All you have to do is keep your inventory stocked at the Amazon warehouse. This can turn into a very lucrative side business that allows you the freedom of running your own businesses and the creativity to make custom products for your client base.

There are plenty of success stories that you can read about on the Handmade homepage. You might even be able to gather some ideas for your own shop. The best part about opting for this type of program is that there are less shops for you to compete with. One-of-a-kind items are often items that customers are willing to pay more money for, so you could find a lot of success in a very short amount of time if you choose the right niche. Take a look at what some of the most successful shops on Handmade are selling; it's the best way to see what kind of items are in demand.

Popular Items in 2019

If you truly don't know where to start, the following are some popular niches that sellers tend to find success with:

Drone Accessories -- Drones are a very high-demand product nowadays, and because they are becoming more and more affordable, a wider variety of people are purchasing them. They are customizable in many ways, so if you stock a shop that has various different accessories, you will likely find some recurring customers.

Posture Correctors -- Everything from seat cushions to neck pillows, posture correctors tend to do very well on Amazon. Because it is so convenient to order these items online, without the customer having to go to a specialty shop, you will likely find it easy to gain clients if you have some of these types of products in your shop.

Phone Cases -- Nearly every single person has a cell phone these days, and most like to keep them protected. Phone cases are relatively inexpensive, and in very high demand. You are almost guaranteed to make a sale if you keep some phone cases in stock.

Pro tip: Don't just go with stock plastic and rubber cases. Funky cases like bamboo, graphite and carbon fiber are all the rage, and you can charge premium prices for them.

LED Lighting -- Customizable lighting features are very trendy right now, and there are products that can appeal to a wide variety of people. This is another fairly inexpensive item that you can keep your shop stocked with. From light bulbs to strip lighting, this is a niche that features plenty of unique finds.

Pros and Cons

It is no secret that Amazon is a huge platform that has continued success all over the world. When you are looking to make an extra income, it makes sense to join a team that is already thriving. With Amazon FBA, you will get a taste of what it is like to run your own business. You also have the option to let your creative side run wild, if you choose.

Pros:

- It Is a Convenient Way to Sell: If you are going to select a platform to sell your items, why not go with one that is already ultra successful? Amazon has already made a name for themselves, so you don't have to work as hard to convince customers that your platform is a reputable one. Your customers will also get all of the traditional perks that other Amazon customers receive. Everything from the packing, shipping, and customer service -- Amazon will take care of it all.
- The Search Algorithm Helps You Advertise: Without even asking for advertisement, Amazon's algorithm takes action. FBA sellers automatically get priority in the search results. This allows you to be seen by more people and gives you the opportunity to gain recurring customers. One of the hardest parts about starting your own business

is informing people about it, and Amazon takes care of this for you automatically.

- Prime Shipping Applies to Your Products: Anyone with a Prime membership will be able to receive your items with Prime shipping. This means that they will get their items faster and with no additional charge. This is just another way that Amazon works in your favor, keeping customer satisfaction up from the very beginning.

- You Can Sell Virtually Anything You Want: With Amazon FBA, you have an unlimited opportunity to sell any product of your choosing. You can stock your store with items that can commonly be ordered in bulk, you can have the opportunity to sell "dangerous" goods like perfume and beauty supplies, you can sell used items that you no longer have a use for, or you can even create your own items. The ball really is in your court when it comes to the selection that you can put into your inventory.

- The Amount of Time You Devote Can Vary: If you just want to put a few items into your store and never stock it again, that would be fine. Or, you can grow your store into a larger entity that always has bulk items in stock. The frequency in which you stock your store is truly up to your own discretion. This type of an online job gives you the flexibility that is essential when you have other things going on in your life. You don't necessarily have to prioritize your store unless you want to.

Cons:

- Costs Can Get High: Having your own Amazon store is a pretty big responsibility. You will need to pay for your account/inventory storage, so keep that in mind before you decide whether opening a store is right for you. Most of the time, people see a return in their investment, but it can take some time. The important thing to remember if you want to stick with it is to be as patient as you can.

- You Must Ship Items to the Warehouse: When you are sending your items to the inventory warehouse, they must be packaged correctly or else Amazon will not accept them. Make sure that you clearly understand all of the guidelines that are in place before you take the time to make a shipment. If you do this part incorrectly, you might have to pay additional fees for Amazon to fix the packaging.

- Delays Can Happen During the Holidays: Amazon is a huge hub when it comes to online gift shopping. During the busiest months of the year, especially around the winter holidays, items that you keep in stock might become unavailable or delayed. If you cannot gain access to these items, you will have to wait until you can restock your own shop. This can be frustrating, especially if you want to participate in the holiday rush.

- You Can't Make Your Own Email List: After you make a sale, you do not have the right to your customer's email address. This isn't necessarily a negative thing, but if you wanted to send out mass emails to existing clients, you wouldn't be able to do so. A lot of business owners like to have this information in order to promote special deals to their existing customers.
- Branding is Out of Your Hands: If you have a vision for your shop that involves a logo, you won't get you use it on your boxes. Unfortunately, using Amazon FBA means that all of your customers will receive standard Amazon packaging in the mail. This isn't a big deal to some, but other business owners might see a certain vision for their company that won't be possible to pursue via FBA.

Kindle Publishing

If you have something to say, why not share it with the world? Kindle Publishing gives a voice to those who write. It is a self-serving platform that writers can utilize in order to publish and sell their work. Once you have some content to work with, you can edit this on Kindle Publishing. With their various tools, you are able to customize your writing to your liking. There is even a chance to create your own book cover if you do not already have one that you are working with. After this, you can decide if you'd like to publish in ebook format or in paperback. Kindle will help you with all of the finer details of publishing. When your book has been published, it will become available for sale on Amazon This platform makes it possible for just about anyone to publish their own work.

While publishing a book can sound like an overwhelming task, it is one that you can easily achieve. This is an excellent way to make a side income, because the book will continue to make you money after you put in all of the work. With Kindle Publishing, you will have plenty of resources and references to use during your writing process. They make publishing as easy as possible; you will be able to focus more on spreading the word about your book than the technicalities involved with creating your content.

What to Write About

Even if you don't consider yourself an "author," there are likely plenty of topics that you are able to write about. Think about what genuinely interests you -- Do you have any passions? What are you knowledgeable about? Would you like to help people? This part can often be the hardest; in a way, it is the process of choosing a niche for your book. When you publish something, you are creating your own personal brand. You need to consider how you would like to present yourself to the audience.

Are you going to come from a self-help writer point of view? Would you like to create a work of fiction? The possibilities are endless, and this period of self-discovery can be very fun. Take as much time as you can to brainstorm all of the different ideas you can write about. Also, write often! Even if you are just writing in a journal, these thoughts can turn into some tangible ideas. You need to be able to be honest with yourself and your own thoughts, as this transparency will allow you to access your best ideas.

Once you have a few topics, set aside some time each week to free-write on these topics. Staying inspired during the writing process can be difficult. Aside from not knowing what to say, you might also find yourself distracted. Ensure that you are giving yourself a fair chance to sit in peace for an hour or so. Unplugging from screens and other electronic devices can be super challenging, especially when they have become such a huge part of our society. The writing process can become very similar to a meditation. Just allow yourself to process your thoughts and ideas, writing them down as you go along. Remember, there is no right or wrong here -- just express yourself!

After you have some content to work with, you can start to refine it. Create a new document and consider it your rough draft. Examine your writing and try to decide if what you are saying is what you would like to convey to the audience. This process can vary for everyone, but using an organized method like this will help you to decide what you'd like to publish. At this point, getting outside opinions can be helpful. If you feel comfortable, bounce some ideas off of family members or friends. You can even join some social media writers' groups to share your work. Getting honest feedback will further refine your content, so be open to what others have to say.

This process is going to take time, and the amount is unknown. Unless you want to set a deadline for yourself, you do not need to stress out over the time it takes to write your content. Some people do it over a year, others can do it in weeks. Keeping a tentative timeline can be handy; this will also provide you with the motivation to push through any writer's block you might experience. The bottom line is that you should always want to make the process enjoyable. If you aren't enjoying what you are doing, then you might need to reevaluate the steps that you are taking.

Is It "Book-Worthy?"

The process of writing a book can often bring up some feelings of self-doubt. You might ask yourself -- "Will anyone even care about this if I publish it?" This feeling is 100% normal! Think about all of the different niches that there are. Thinking about any topic and you will be able to do an Amazon search and find a book on it. If you are worried about your audience not being receptive to your work, the focus should actually be on who you are marketing to rather than what you are marketing. Try your best to boost your morale as often as you can.

Remind yourself that publishing your own work is a huge accomplishment and that your hard work will pay off. This can be hard to realize when you are still in the developmental stage of pre-publishing.

Having a support system can be great to alleviate any doubts that might come up. Even if you aren't sharing your work with others, you can tell those closest to what you are up to. Talk about your goals and why you are working hard to publish your work. This support will boost you whenever you are feeling down, and it will help you whenever you have those moments when you feel like giving up. These feelings are bound to come up, so don't stress over them too much.

On a more statistical note, if you are worried about sales, then you can spend a little bit more time doing research before you begin your rough draft. Take a look at the current literary trends. What kind of books are on the bestseller lists right now? Do any of these topics appeal to you? Talk to your friends, too! What kinds of books do they enjoy reading? Anything that is being purchased frequently can be considered a current "trending topic." While these topics can change often, it might help you decide on which direction that you'd like to take your writing.

For another entirely different approach, you can write about something unique that isn't trending. If you have something that you'd like to write about that isn't currently on the charts, go for it! Adding a niche to a market can be a risk, but it might pay off because there aren't many others like it in the same category. Remember, you get to determine what is "book-worthy," not the audience. Even if you do not see a lot of immediate sales, you can work extra hard to market your content to the right people.

Whether you are an experienced writer or you are new to the field, these self-doubting tendencies can creep up at any point in time. By knowing how to boost your confidence in a healthy way, you will be able to overcome these feelings and continue with your publishing process. Talking with others who are in the same boat can also be essential to overcoming any worries you have. As was mentioned, there are many existing groups online that revolve around the writing and publishing process. Becoming a part of one gives you the chance to vent and bounce ideas off of like-minded people.

Not a writer? No problem.

There are many ghostwriting companies who will write your book for you after you submit an outline. This obviously costs more, but saves you a ton of time and effort.

Prices start from $1.50/100 words, so a 12,000 word non-fiction book will set you back around $180.

Popular companies include

http://theurbanwriters.com and http://ewritersolutions.com

Cover Appearance

As you are making progress with writing your content, you should also be thinking about branding. What do you want your book cover to look like? This part can seem overwhelming to beginners, but you have plenty of options thanks to Kindle Publishing:

Hire Someone -- You can hire someone to create your book cover. Even if you have no idea where to begin, hiring an artist or graphic designer to create the cover for you is a great first step. After you decide on someone that you would like to work with, you will likely have a consultation that will allow you to come up with some ideas. Do you want your cover to be cohesive with your title? Do you have a different vision?

Draw It -- If you consider yourself a capable artist, you can create your own cover! Taking your art and turning into a digital image is one way for you to create your own cover art. You will be able to upload it onto Kindle Publishing and customize the font using the Cover Creator tool after that.

Use the Tools -- Something in between drawing the cover art yourself and utilizing help from others is using digital images and then customizing the cover on Kindle. You can take art that has already been created (with permission) and then use it to build your book cover. The great thing about Kindle is that they give you these tools for free.

This part is creative and fun! It allows you to decide what visual image you would like to use to represent your written work. If you start thinking about this while you are still writing, this will give you plenty of time to bring it into fruition before it is time to publish. Remember, this part can be changed or customized. If you finish writing and then you realize that your cover doesn't truly represent the work or doesn't fit the niche, you can change it.

For an ebook, creating the cover is simple and does not require much editing. You will decide what you would like it to look like and what it should say. The measurements aren't as big of a deal since the content is going to be visual. When you are deciding on a cover for a physical paperback book, you will need to make sure that your cover art fits the Kindle guidelines. Luckily, Kindle will not allow you to publish anything that doesn't meet the requirements. They will assist you with any resizing that needs to be done. You will also have options to decide on paper color and finish.

Even if you have no experience with creating a book cover, Kindle makes it easy for those of all skill levels. If you have any specific questions, there is also a great guide that has been complied with several FAQs that have been asked (and answered) by other writers. You should be able to do this all yourself with the help of these resources. Alternatively, if you are using a graphic designer to design the cover, you can talk about the sizing with them ahead of time to make sure that everything is going to meet the guidelines.

Submitting Your Work

Once you have your content and cover ready for publishing, Kindle will guide you through the final steps. Uploading all of your work is as simple as the click of a button. If anything must be changed before the final publishing, Kindle will inform you of what that is. Their system is intended to be very transparent, so you are as prepared as you can be. When you upload your manuscript, it should already be it its final form, fully edited. The Kindle system will do a light scan of it to further ensure that there are no additional errors.

The same process will happen with your cover art. Depending on if you are releasing an ebook or a paperback, Kindle will update you accordingly with what must be done in order to meet all of the standard requirements. As mentioned, uploading the cover art for an ebook is easier due to the fact that it remains digital. A paperback will be distributed physically, so the quality must be higher in order to ensure that your book is going to look as professional as possible.

Once all of your work has been uploaded, you get to fill in basic fields such as title and description. These fields are what will be displayed on your Amazon product page, so make sure that you are accurately representing your work in a detailed fashion. Kindle then gives you the option to select certain categories for your work, for example: Fiction, Non-Fiction, Poetry, History, etc...The options are endless, so try your best to select the 3 that best represent your writing.

Pricing is further explained during this stage of publication. Kindle offers two different royalty programs. There are benefits that can be explained in greater detail, but they offer plans that provide you either 35% or 70% of the money to you as the author; Kindle keeps a percentage, too. There are certain qualifiers that must be met to qualify for the 70% royalty program, so do some research before you make your final selection.

Once all of these details are chosen, you will submit everything to Kindle and then wait for the approval. Normally, approval is decided pretty quickly (24-72 hours). If anything must be changed, you will receive an email with these requests. Once you receive your approval, it can take up to 72 more hours for your book to appear in the Amazon store. This is an exciting moment for all writers; it takes all of that hard work that you have put in and turns it into something tangible that you can be proud of.

Spreading the Word

Once your title is available on the Amazon Marketplace, you can feel free to talk about it on every platform that you are a part of. Make posts about it on social media, tell friends and family, and do anything else that you see fit in order to get the word out. Remember that being proud about something you worked hard on is nothing to feel embarrassed about; you must generate some noise in order to get the sales started. Users can organically come across your title on Amazon, but doing your own independent marketing will bring you even more success.

If you want to give your book an even bigger publicity boost, you can pay for some basic advertising. Nearly any app has the option now to utilize pay-per-click advertising. Whether you choose to do this directly on Amazon, or from your social media accounts, you can compile a post that will target certain audiences. Doing this will create even more buzz about your title. Each additional person that buys your book is another opportunity for word-of-mouth advertising. This is exactly how it sounds -- When someone buys your book and talks about it with other people, this is "word of mouth."

Giveaways are a great tactic to use when you are releasing something new. Offering a copy of your work for free can generate curiosity about the book. Amazon provides you with ways to set up your own giveaway. You get to pick the algorithm and the amount of winners, a fully customizable experience. This tool is always available to you as a writer on Amazon. If you feel that you ever need to re-generate the buzz about your work, try doing a giveaway! This will also feature your product on the Amazon Giveaways homepage, yet another way for your work to get noticed by people who are browsing.

Getting ratings on Amazon is a free way that you can boost your sales. Verified ratings of your work will help others to determine if they would like to give it a read or not. Encourage your customers to leave a rating and a review once they have read your work. This is a great thing that you can ask of your friends and family members who are likely willing to vouch for you. Books with higher ratings do better on the Amazon charts and are boosted on the algorithms. Try your best to obtain as many ratings as possible from your readers.

You need to be strategic with your advertising plan. Of course, you want your book to be successful with a lot of sales, but don't get caught up in spending too much money on advertising. If you are purchasing ads every week, you might end up spending more than you are making. Another thing to keep in mind that you are not going to get paid by Kindle instantly. That part takes time, so factoring this into your budget is essential if you are just starting out as a self-published writer.

When Will You Get Paid?

As you begin your journey as a writer on Kindle/Amazon, you will have to provide your bank account information, or an alternative way to get paid. Direct deposit to your bank account is the easiest way for you to get your money quickly. You will also need to fill out your tax information, because being a self-published writer involves paying takes, just like any other standard job. You can expect to see your first paycheck 60 days after the end of your first month's sales. This is the payment schedule that Amazon follows for royalty payments.

Imaginably, doing this for a side income does involve a lot of patience and effort, but you can just as easily become very successful. This type of job will pay for itself over time, and as long as your book stays on the market with sales, you can expect to see a continual paycheck. This is why marketing is essential after you release written work. You need to keep your audience engaged with and excited about your book in order to keep generating sales. This part can require some creativity on your end. Think about ways that you can advertise that would naturally catch your own eye.

A big component to being successful as a self-published writer is luck. It does take luck to get noticed sometimes. No matter how hard you work, selling a book requires you to have a willing audience. If you find that certain marketing approaching aren't really generating many sales, you can try different ones. The whole process will likely be a bit of trial and error until you can determine what works the best. Once you get into the flow of marketing and selling, you will see your royalties flowing in without a problem.

Pros and Cons

If being an author has ever seemed out of reach, Kindle Direct is here to prove you wrong. With all of the tools that you will need for self-publishing, you can work with Kindle to turn your ideas into a literary reality. This process can be both exciting and practical – Many people find that their books sell themselves.

Pros:

- You Will Be A Part of the Largest Ebook Market: Through the Kindle/Amazon marketplace, several authors find success when publishing their written work. Because the market is so large, there is a niche for just about anything. This means that you will likely find success, as long as you are able to find the right marketing techniques.

- You Can Sell Worldwide: Because Amazon is accessible by people all around the globe, your book can be, too. Without ever having to leave your computer, you are able to make sales in several different countries. This instant-access type of market is great, especially if you are just starting out in the industry.

- The System is Simple: Even if you have never published written work before, the step-by-step process makes it easy for you to do everything that you need. The need to hire an outside source isn't necessary unless you choose to. From editing to creating cover art, you can do it all on the Kindle Publishing website.

- Amazon Has Built-In Marketing Tools: From ads to giveaways, there are plenty of chances for you to promote your product. You can easily set your marketing up from your Amazon author page, and it will give your content the boost that it deserves. The best part is, there are no additional fees to use these services.

- Get Your Money Directly to Your Bank Account: Direct deposit is an option that you can choose for your royalty payments. Just like any traditional job, you can report and receive your income the same way. This is a lucrative job that is well-respected and will serve you well if you put in the effort.
- Leverage the ever-growing audiobook market. Amazon owns Audible, and thus, after you get your book narrated, you can upload it onto there as well. If you have a book in a popular niche, then it's not uncommon to make $1,000 a month on Audible alone.

Cons:

- It Takes Time to Get Paid: Not only do you need to make sure that you are making sales, but when you do make them, it takes up to 60 days for you to see that profit. Unfortunately, this is just the system that Amazon has in place for sending you royalty payments. If you are looking for instant gratification, then self-publishing likely isn't going to be right for you.
- Writing Takes a Lot of Preparation: Writing a book is a big deal! You are going to need to put in a lot of prep work before you are able to enjoy any of the benefits. This involves: coming up with a concept, writing drafts, editing the final outcome, putting together the publishing details, and more. If this is something that you truly enjoy doing, then writing a book should not be a problem for you. As long as it is enjoyable, you should have the motivation to keep pushing forward.
- Marketing Can Be Difficult: Talking about your book is something that you might need to practice, but it is necessary if you want to make sales. You will need to choose how you would like to represent yourself, and make social media posts that reflect this. Advertising on your own this way is one of the most common sources for self-published authors. For one, it is free, so you won't have to worry about spending more than you make. You just need to be willing to put in the time to think about creative ways to get the word out about your book.

- You Will Have a Lot of Competition: While your book will be for sale on the biggest digital marketplace in the world, that also means that you will have a lot of direct competition. It can be hard to get noticed when there are so many other writers out there that are self-publishing and using Kindle/Amazon as a platform.
- You'll Need to Keep Momentum Going: There is a lot of buzz that surrounds a newly released book. Once this energy dies down, it is up to you to keep customers interested in buying your work. This part can be a bit discouraging at times, and you need to develop the determination necessary to not give up when you are no longer seeing sales.

Ecommerce Agency

Ecommerce is a topic that should already be familiar to you -- Instead of stocking and selling products online, you can actually work in ecommerce as an assistant to businesses that are already up and running. An ecommerce agent's job is to boost sales for ecommerce shops. Every online business must market their products in order to make sales, and it can be your job to help with this process. In a couple of simple steps, you can get online businesses to pay you for helping them grow in the marketplace.

How to Select Which Business to Work With

As a consumer, you should already have a basic idea of the kinds of stores that exist online. You probably purchase items online on a regular basis. Before you begin your job as an ecommerce agent, you should consider which types of businesses are in demand. Remember, the selection process works both ways -- the business will survey you just as much as you survey it. A good starting point is to determine if said business has a product that people will actually want to buy. While finding a specialty clock store online might be unique, it likely won't be as successful as a modern watch store. You just need to use your common sense to figure out if spending the time to work with a business is going to be beneficial.

This is a chance for you to really zone in on what you are interested in; do some research in some of the industries that appeal to you. Just about anything and everything can be purchased online, so it shouldn't be hard to find some stores that appeal to you. As you are narrowing down your options, keep in mind how realistic the products being sold are. Is there going to be a use for them now? A few years down the road? You will want to consider the future. Selecting a dying industry can be a huge mistake and will put an end to your side income.

Once you have your eyes set on a couple of businesses, take a look at the way they represent themselves online. This is essential in the field of ecommerce. Make sure that they have a website that is updated and functional. Also, take a look at their social media presence. A business that already cares about both of these aspects is going to be a lot easier to represent and promote. While it is going to be your job to make sure that they keep up with their online marketing activity, you shouldn't have to put in 100% of the work.

Getting Noticed

Once you have some potential clients to work with, one of the most important steps comes next -- You have to bridge the gap. The following are some strategies that you can utilize to approach these businesses:

- Draft an email: Before you make contact with a company, you should determine what you are going to say. You'll want your approach to be the right amount of professional, but also friendly. Of course, if you are working for an ecommerce agency, the agency itself should also be able to guide you through this process.
- Eliminate any spam dialogue: When you are about to send your initial email, read over it to make sure that none of it sounds like spam. Think about if you were to get the email as a business owner -- Would you read it or delete it? If the content does not sound natural, you might want to rethink your approach. Remember, your initial email should be a conversation starter rather than a sales pitch.
- Be transparent: In your email, you will want to explain exactly what services that you will provide to the business. There should be no guesswork done by the owner. Talk about how you can help the business grow and what tactics you will use to get it to that point.
- Discuss pricing: Some find it taboo to talk about pricing right away, but bringing it up from the start can save you a lot of time. If a business owner does not agree with your price point, it is better to know right away than wasting your time going back and forth with negotiations. Set your price and stand firmly where you set it. You need to have confidence in the services that you provide and the amount that you deserve to be paid. If you are working with an ecommerce agency, there will usually be predetermined prices that you must charge.
- Point out their flaws: This is not meant to insult the business, but if you notice that the website could use improvement, include that detail in your pitch. Acknowledging the existing marketing that a business has in place not only shows that you are actively thinking about how you can make it better, but it also shows your involvement from the start. Taking a few minutes to look at a business's online presence will allow you

to sound more professional as you initiate contact and provide recommendations. This gives the business owner an idea of the what the future holds by working with you. Being able to imagine real results is a great push for why that business should hire you.

How Much to Charge

If you are starting your own ecommerce agency, one of the hardest things to decide is what to charge for your services. Especially when you are just starting out, it can be difficult for you to put a value on what you can do for other businesses. It is recommended that agencies start with a minimum of $1,000 per month for each business that they help. This might be well above the amount that you were originally thinking, but it is a well-justified starting figure. A big mistake that is often made by ecommerce agencies is charging too little for their services.

When your prices are too low, customers might begin to take advantage of you. They might become needy or demanding, and the work will eventually outweigh the profit. You will want to make sure that you are paid comfortably for all the services provided. The odds are that 1 out of every 10 clients will say yes. You will have to get used to the idea that there will be rejection. Some might even point out that your pricing is too high, but if you know your worth, you will be able to stand firm and continue to the next prospect.

There are some exceptions: If you are working with a business that wants to recommend a friend who becomes another client, giving the original business a discount would be a nice sort of referral system. You would be gaining more clientele, so it would still be considered a gain for you. This type of mindset is important when you are entering the ecommerce industry. You need to be strategic and detailed, always one step ahead of the game.

Another incentive for standing firm with your price point is the fact that this is a side job for you. While you probably already have a main source of income, you won't have to rely on this money in order to live. Having an additional income means having an extra source of money that should essentially be easy to obtain. If you find yourself putting in more work than what your money's worth is, you might want to reconsider whether you are charging enough.

Know How to Operate the Business

Much like any other job, you will have to do some training in order to succeed. Whether you begin working for an existing agency or you decide to start your own, having basic ecommerce knowledge is essential for the future of your success. The secret to being good at your job is knowing how to do all of the various tasks that come with it. You will need to know how to set up an ecommerce shop. The easiest way to do this will be by utilizing a platform, such as Shopify. If you need practice, set up your own test shop so that you are familiar with the steps.

If you are able to walk a business owner through something, your skills will be considered more valid. By placing a business on Shopify, you are helping them branch out. Assuming they do not already have a Shopify account in place, you can begin by setting one up for your client. With your knowledge about the platform, it can be your job to set up, maintain, and monitor this online shop. Because Shopify is so easy to use, it is frequently going to be a great starting point when you are working with ecommerce.

Having basic knowledge about web design is also going to strengthen your skills as an ecommerce agent. This can be learned by doing some reading and by creating and editing your own websites. Remember, you are going to be aiming to work with ecommerce businesses that already have decent websites in place, but you might need to perform a little bit of maintenance from time to time. You will always want to stress how important having a functional website is. Potential customers see a business website as a portal for how the owner runs the company.

If a website is hard to navigate, the business will likely lose clients due simply to lack of organization. It is your job as an agent to streamline this. Even if the website itself has decent content and updated HTML, you might need to suggest a little bit of clean-up work. Think about what you can do for the website in order to make the browsing experience as pleasant as possible. Making sure that the customers can see all of the products offered and easily make a purchase is going to be one of the main components of your job.

Encourage your clients to aim for innovative marketing strategies. People like to see visual representation when they shop. Are there enough photos on the website and with the product listings? Is there a chance for the customer to see a video that corresponds with the products? Small steps like this can make a huge difference in customer engagement. Your aim is to grab the attention of these customers to turn the intrigue into sales. Think about what would impress you if you were browsing on the website. What would make the client select the given business to make their purchase?

There is a fine line between creating a spark and coming off as a gimmick, so be wary when you are making suggestions to your client. You will want to be interesting enough to draw attention to the shop, but not be perceived over the top. This type of balance can often take practice, but you will quickly learn what works and what does not work in your given industry. Being in the ecommerce field does take a little trial and error.

Never make promises to your client that you cannot keep. Telling a client that their business is going to grow by 500% in a month is not realistic. Make sure to keep up with the transparency, even after you are hired. It is your job to work together with the business to form strategies that will draw in business. If something isn't working as well as you planned, go back to the drawing board and try again. You will want to encourage the business owner to try new things, because sometimes, people will overlook the same old marketing strategies.

Get Them Customers

Helping a business grow means you are essentially going to help them make sales. This becomes possible by gaining clients, and that is where your help comes in. An ecommerce agent makes it a point to effectively market the business in order to gain the attention of the customers. You need to effectively convince customers why they are making the right choice, and this can be done by using a few different methods:

- SEO Keywords: Make sure that the business website is SEO-formatted. What this means is that whenever a potential customer makes a search online using designated keywords, the business will come up near the top of the search results. By doing this, you are allowing the consumer to make a quick selection. Nobody likes to search for hours when they are in need of something simple. Being near the top of the search will likely earn that business customers by way of convenience. You can get higher rankings in search engines by adding the keywords customers are most likely to use when searching for your products to the ecommerce site's web copy.

- Hold a Sale: Listing a product for sale might increase the likelihood of visitors finding the ecommerce shop. Everyone likes getting discounted items, and while they are browsing, they might even find other products that they would be willing to buy.

Having a sale every so often keeps the business engagement up.

- Put a Code on Social Media: This tactic kills two birds with one stone -- Provide a discount code on social media that customers can use on the website. This will not only encourage people to follow the social media pages, but it will also attract visitors to the website. Again, people love to save money whenever possible. Giving out a discount code to a select audience promotes a sense of exclusivity.

- Start a Blog: Companies that have blogs on their websites allow customers to see the more personal side of the business. A blog is a great way for the business owner to introduce their staff and give potential customers an inside look as to how the business operates. Adding a blog to the website will not cost the business any money, and it will be an additional source for advertisement and promotion. It is a great way to connect with customers with no added hassle. SEO keywords can also be utilized in blogs, so keep that in mind when they are being written.

- Make the Online Presence Beautiful: If a website is eye-catching, it will attract more visitors. Encourage the business that you are working with to team up with a graphic designer who can create cohesive logos and branding. This is an important, and often overlooked, step to owning a business. When things have a sense of cohesiveness, people feel more inclined to trust said business. This is also a reflection of the way the business chooses to stay organized.

- Email Lists: Getting people to sign up for a mailing list is a handy tool when it comes to marketing. When a business is able to stay in touch with their clients, they have a bigger chance of making a recurring sale. The mailing list can be a way for customers to receive exclusive deals or obtain early access to certain products. Encourage the business to stay on top of their list, sending out correspondence on a regular basis.

- Offer Free Samples: If it makes sense, sending out free samples of products could entice customers to make purchases. This is also a great way to convince people to sign up for a mailing list. People will not want to turn down a free product, so this can be a great way to quickly and effectively generate client outreach.

Why Ecommerce is a Successful Industry

When you seek a secondary income, it is important that you select an industry that is on the rise. This means, you want to choose a job that will be useful and in demand. Ecommerce has been a successful industry for quite some time now. Ever since the internet advanced in such ways that consumers were easily able to make purchases, the ecommerce marketplace saw major spikes in activity.

Not to mention, having a side income also means that you will probably have only a little bit of time to devote to this additional job. Ecommerce is all run online, and this is perfect for someone who already has plenty of in-person responsibilities. Consider how often you utilize the internet in your daily life -- this is why a job in ecommerce can become a successful source for you to make money.

The hardest part about this job is getting noticed by businesses and gaining their trust. It does take skill and creativity in order to figure out how to get the response that you are looking for, but with enough practice, it becomes easy. Much like other jobs, you need to ensure that you are creating a real connection with your potential clients. Treat every interaction with the same level of professionalism that you would expect to receive. This industry has a "snowball" effect; once you are in contact with the right people, the work falls into your lap.

Technology is not something that shows any signs of slowing down any time soon. As a society, we become more and more dependent on it as the years go on. You will be able to secure a future with a job in ecommerce, because it has proven to be useful for such a long stretch of time. As long as you are willing to put in the effort, you can reach any level of success that you desire.

Pros and Cons

Ecommerce isn't a new industry -- in fact, it has been popular for several decades now. Helping other businesses thrive can in turn become a great business for you to make extra money on the side. The task isn't as complicated as it seems. If you are willing to do some hands-on research, you can make a successful additional career for yourself from the comfort of your own computer.

Pros:

- You Have a Potential for Growth: You can begin by working for a single business, and eventually, you can take on more clients. Being an ecommerce agent gives you the ability to decide on your own level of work. If you need more to do, take on more clients! This freedom and potential are available to you from the very beginning.

- You Will Be a Part of a Top Industry: Getting a leading industry job can be difficult in most cases, but with ecommerce, you can get started with minimal experience. Unlike many other positions in ecommerce, you won't need a degree to work as an ecommerce agent. This means that you can choose to become a part of the industry at any given moment that you decide you want to start earning more money.
- Meeting New People Is a Perk: By approaching different businesses that you would like to work with, you will be building up your online social network. This is a way for you to meet a lot of new people in a short amount of time. Expanding your circle is beneficial both in a professional setting and a personal one. You might connect with businesses that you normally would not have, all thanks to your outreach.
- The Money Can Multiply: Once you get the hang of what it takes to be an ecommerce agent, you might find yourself available to take on more work. Remember, the more clients you have, the more money that you will be able to secure. As long as you are able to deliver your promised services, you will see successful results.
- You Get to Communicate With Others Frequently: If you consider yourself a people person, then ecommerce is a great side job to choose. One of the main tasks that you will have to do is communicate with others. Creating meaningful and honest connections with people is what makes for a good ecommerce agent. People can see past lies and gimmicks, even on the internet. If you can persuade customers to purchase products in an honest way, then you know that your skills are top notch.

Cons:

- There Is a Lot of Competition: Much like yourself, plenty of other people have probably seen what a great opportunity working in ecommerce can be. You will need to find ways to set yourself apart from the rest. Think about what makes you unique and what special skills you have to offer. Don't get discouraged if you do not get a job right away. Remember, one in every 10 people normally say yes.

- Pressure Is a Part of the Job: You are going to be expected to meet goals. Namely, you are going to be expected to generate sales for the business that you are working with. If this is something that you do not think you can handle or accomplish, then the ecommerce industry isn't the right industry for you. Being able to go with the flow is essential for working in a job like this.

- Getting Started Is the Hardest Part: You are going to need to do some preparation before you are able to serve businesses. Having knowledge about running an ecommerce store is one factor. The other is being able to approach businesses and convince them to hire you. The ease of these steps depends on if you are starting your own agency or working for an existing agency. Working for an existing agency might provide you with more training resources.

- Contracts Can End After Time: When you start working for a business, you might generate so much success for them that they will no longer see a need for your services. This is okay; it happens! The goal is to always have clients lined up to work with. When you become too comfortable in what you are currently doing, you might end up at a dead end. Being proactive about your work is the key to staying relevant in the industry.

- You Might Not Know How Much You Deserve: As discussed, it can be hard to give someone a price for your services, especially when you are new to the industry. You must work on your confidence when you are discussing budgets with your clients. Stand firm in your pricing, and those who are serious about working with you will make themselves known. You have to know that your pricing is a direct correlation to your skill set, and it is not wrong to want to be well compensated. This is what makes being an ecommerce agent an online side hustle.

Freelance Copywriting

Do you have a knack for selling with words? Utilizing your skills as a freelance copywriter could be a great potential source of additional income! No matter what the topic is, writers often seek outside help when it comes to making sure that their work is up to the correct standards. By working as a freelancer, you will have the opportunity to help writers on your own time. You will get to choose what jobs sound interesting to you and when you would like to work on them. This flexibility is what makes freelance copywriting one of the most popular side hustles that you can succeed in.

Freedom of Choice

Being a freelancer is one of the most flexible careers that you can choose. Normally, there are aspects of your day job that you most likely don't care to do. With freelancing, you get to pick which projects sound most interesting to you. There are several different deciding factors when it comes to taking on freelancing projects. If you are utilizing a website to find jobs, you will likely be able to use certain criteria to narrow down your search. Before you apply for these jobs, think about what interests you the most.

Once you have an idea of the topics you'd be willing to write about or edit, you can make customized searches. When you are trying to make an additional income, you have way more freedom of choice. This money is like bonus money, and that's the best part about it -- you have the ability to be selective. By only writing about topics that interest you, it is likely that the quality of your work will be much better than if you were writing about randomly assigned topics.

Alternatively, being a freelancer also means that you can be open to a wider range of tasks. It is truly up to your own personal preference. If you don't mind what you are going to be writing about, keep those search parameters open. Because you will continuously get different jobs, the work assigned to you will vary. Keeping your job interesting will encourage your creativity to flow.

Other than choosing which topics you want to write about, you also have the freedom to take on or pass up a job offer based on the employer. Applying for a freelancing job opens the lines of communication for both parties involved. You will get the chance to interview the employer in the same way that you get interviewed. Remember, this is not your full-time job. You should only work with those who you see true potential in. Don't feel bad for passing up offers that seem like more trouble than they are worth. Most freelancing jobs are temporary, so make sure that you are using your time wisely.

Negotiating Payments

At a traditional job, you are normally paid by the hour or with a salary. These norms are entirely different when it comes to freelancing. Generally, you will get paid per job when you freelance. This happens because you will likely work for several different people in a short period of time. Along with your freedom of choice when it comes to the jobs that you choose, you also get to have flexibility with the amount of money you earn.

When you are starting a freelance copywriting job, there will be an initial conversation with the employer. You will normally discuss the topic at hand and what the employer expects you to deliver. If you both feel that you meet all of the requirements, then you get to talk about price points. They will likely have an amount in mind, and you have the right to make suggestions on it. If you feel that the work is worth more than the amount being offered, ask for more money!

Think about your work as a freelancer as something that you don't need, but instead, something that you are actively choosing. You have the right to redefine your worth, and if the employer is not willing to pay you what you are asking, then you can politely decline the job. Many freelancers are scared to ask for what they actually think they deserve, but it just takes some practice. After some time, you will notice that your employers will respect you more if you are standing up for what you believe is fair.

Suggesting a price point is also a good way to weed out employers that are going to give you trouble. For example, if someone would like you to assist with copywriting a long novel for only $10, you will likely be over-exerting yourself for very little profit. Suggest that the budget be changed, and if the answer is no, you can move on to the next project. By establishing this boundary from the start of your career, you won't waste your time on draining projects that underpay.

Another example of a job that is troublesome is when the employer nitpicks your work without offering helpful suggestions. If someone is only going to pick apart what you worked hard on, with no clear conclusion in sight, this might be a job that you are going to want to pass up. Know that your time and efforts are just as valuable as anyone else's. This job is meant to supply you with additional income, and it shouldn't be causing you extreme amounts of stress or pressure.

If you don't know where to begin on fair pricing, think about an hourly rate that you think is fair. Also, you might want to consider what rate you think is fair per 100 words. With these two things in mind, you will be able to determine if the employer falls within your "fair pricing" range. All of this is a matter of opinion, but if you take a look at what some other freelancers normally charge, you might be able to gather some ideas for your own work.

Third-Party Websites

Anyone can be a freelance copywriter, but it is helpful to utilize online resources in order to put yourself ahead. The following are some ways you can give yourself a platform on which to get noticed as a freelancer:

- Upwork: This site is a hub for freelancers to connect with employers. You are able to sign up for a free account, get verified, and get started with working immediately after that. While Upwork is filled with all kinds of work, you are able to search for jobs that are a fit for your skills. So, if you excel in writing and editing, you can put this in your profile. By browsing through various job postings, you can get an idea of what work is available. This changes regularly, so make sure that you are checking Upwork frequently. Once you see some jobs that appeal to you, send a proposal. This is as simple as clicking a button -- You get to say a few words to the employer, and you can attach some writing samples if you have any. If the employer sees potential, they will set up an interview. It is during this process that you get to talk about the scope of the work and the amount that will be paid. Just as simple as this, you could get hired to work on the job. Sometimes, once the contract is over, the employer will end it. Other times, it can remain open and active, in case more work comes up in the future from that same employer. There is a lot you can do on Upwork, and as a freelancer, it can help your career flourish.

  Pro-tip: Initially there looks like a lot of competition on Upwork. But if you niche down, you can easily charge high prices off the bat. For example, there are thousands of profiles listed as "copywriter", yet less than 10 with "Amazon copywriter" or "ClickFunnels Landing Page Copywriter"

- Monster: This is a general website for getting hired. You are able to create a profile and browse through thousands of job listings in your area. While it is not specifically tailored to freelancing, using Monster is a great way to expand your professional network. Because it has been around for such a long time, it is very well known. You will be able to search through freelance jobs, and apply for the ones that interest you most. A level of trust already exists between employers and future employees, because the platform is already well established. It is most likely that you are going to only find credible jobs that are posted on Monster, and this is important when you will be searching the listings frequently.

- Your Personal Website: Another approach to freelancing is to represent yourself. Creating your own website and promoting your skills is possible and a valid way to obtain jobs. Because you will be creating your own content, you will get to decide how you are represented. You can share as little or as much information about yourself as you'd like. As long as you are good with frequently checking your emails, running your own website to find jobs should not be an issue. While the customization features are a plus, remember that you might not get noticed as easily or as quickly when you are trying to freelance solo.
- There are several other websites that you can utilize as you search for jobs as a freelance copywriter. The best part is, you don't necessarily have to stick with just one! You can create your own website while still browsing through sites like Upwork and Monster. The more representation you have, the better your chances will be of earning jobs. With freelancing, the success that you see is very much dependent on the amount of work that you are willing to put in. Not only do you have to deliver as a copywriter, but you also need to become an expert at selling yourself. When you work in freelancing, you are the product that is being advertised. The skills that you have to offer will help clients to decide if they would like to work with you.

Gain Entrepreneur Skills

Being a freelance copywriter means that you will be wearing a lot of hats. You will have to come up with an idea of how to present yourself to others while highlighting your best skills. Then, you will have to live up to this promise and deliver the work discussed. The process continues and repeats for as long as you are willing to commit to it. This is one of the quickest ways to gain experience as an entrepreneur. Working for yourself is a great experience that can teach you a lot. All of the decision-making will be in your hands, and you will get to see the direct results of the choices that you make.

Once you get into the habit of representing yourself, this could lead to bigger opportunities in the future. Being a freelancer shows that you have the self-discipline necessary to get the work done because you want to, not because you have someone overseeing your actions. It provides you with a way to display your independence proudly, while also getting paid to do so! This is a positive experience, and many freelancers agree that they love the freedom that comes with the job.

Sometimes, it can be hard to stay motivated when it comes to working. Try easing into your workload to start. This way, you won't become overwhelmed. The great thing about choosing your own projects is that there are no limits; there is no such thing as not doing enough work. Earning a secondary income should feel this way! Once you feel that you have a grasp on the work, apply for some more jobs. Being a freelancer involves some trial and error, but only you will know what works best for your own schedule. Consider what other obligations you have, and only apply for jobs that you know will fit around them.

You will find that your organizational skills are going to come in handy as you start applying for these freelance copywriting jobs. Not only will you need to have the time to interact with your potential employers, but you will also need to make sure that you can get the work done in the allotted time. This is also something can can be negotiated between yourself and your employer. If you don't think that the given deadline is realistic, propose a new one! Being able to completely organize your workload will give you a great sense of control over the situation. You will know what is happening and when it is happening.

How to Build Your Reputation

When you are first starting out in a new field, one of the toughest parts can be establishing your reputation. Being a freelancer means working on your own time and finding your own projects. This also means that it is up to you to make clients take you seriously. This can seem like a difficult task, especially when you don't have a college degree on the topic. This is okay, though! Even newbies are able to find success by working as freelance copywriters. In order to gain experience, you must put in the work. Take jobs that vary from different topics and different clients.

By adding some variety to your list of work completed, you will be able to show future clients what you are capable of. A lot of employers will ask you for writing samples. This doesn't always need to be published work. If you have ever written any kind of essay before, you might be able to utilize it as a writing sample. Most employers just want to ensure that you are able to clearly piece together your sentences, and they want to know that you have great attention to detail. If you don't have anything written yet, picking a topic and writing 500 words on it could be helpful to add to your portfolio.

No matter what you are writing about, those who are looking at the quality of your work will be able to see a real example. This is how you boost trust with your clients. Eventually, as you work on more jobs, you will have more writing samples to provide to other employers. Many people are under the misconception that you cannot be a freelance copywriter unless you went to school for it. Nowadays, that isn't the case. Clients will hire you if you can present yourself in a trustworthy manner and if you can prove your skills.

Ask clients to leave you reviews and testimonials. On third-party websites, there is usually the option for both the client and yourself to review one another. This is a chance to express how it was to work with one another. Having other people vouch for you is a great indication of your skills and professionalism. If you are running your own website, including these testimonials on your site is a way to entice others to work with you, too. It can be nerve-wracking to ask for constructive criticism, but in the end, this is what will help you with building your reputation.

Writing For Blogs

When you are searching for work as a freelancer, consider approaching different blogs that you would like to be featured on. Plenty of blogs require outside help with writing and editing, so if you have any that you would like to work with, reach out! You will have nothing to lose by reaching out to someone who you want to collaborate with. The worst thing that can happen is they will say no, and then you can just move on and focus on the next task.

By copywriting for blogs that are already well established, you are furthering your career as a freelancer. This is a way for you to get your name out there to an audience that is guaranteed. If the readers respond well to your posts, you might be able to secure a regular job. Being a freelancer does involve a bit of risk-taking, but in the end, it can lead you to some pretty great opportunities. A lot of freelancers partner with blogs in order to gain momentum in their careers. If you aren't sure about joining a third party job site, starting by reaching out to some of your favorite blogs can be another way to enter the industry.

This is another way for you to work on a project-by-project basis. Writing for a blog normally does not involve any contracts to sign, so you will be able to keep your freedom. There are plenty of niches to choose from when it comes to blogs, so a little bit of brainstorming might be required on your end. Think about what you would most enjoy writing about. Do you like to inform people? Help people? Entertain people? The options are nearly endless.

Pros and Cons

When you have a keen eye, it just makes sense to put those skills to use. Freelance copywriters are in high demand for a lot of different projects. This can be quick side work for you to complete when you need some extra money to fill in the gaps. The more effort that you put into freelancing, the better results you will see.

Pros:

- Zero money needed to start: All you need is an internet connection. Even if you have no experience, you can start by reading copywriting blogs and advice on http://thegaryhalbertletter.com (Gary was considered the best copywriter alive for over 2 decades, and he has hundreds of articles available for free on his website). Another useful resource is Ben Settle's email list at http://bensettle.com

- Take on Work When You Need It: As a freelance copywriter, you get to decide if you'd like to work or not. Because the jobs are normally on a temporary basis, you can take on a couple of jobs when you'd like to have a little bit of extra money. If you are too busy to work more jobs, you don't need to apply for more. The system is pretty black and white; it works for a lot of people because of this reason.

- You Can Be Selective: Being picky is encouraged when you are doing any type of freelance work. Because the work does not last for a long period of time, you will need to make sure that you truly get along with the client. Make sure that you both understand the same vision and agree on the same price point. Being selective helps to ensure that your job as a freelancer is enjoyable.

- You'll Learn New Things: It is inevitable that you will be writing about topics you do not know much about yet. This is when your job also becomes a learning opportunity. By working on a piece of writing, you might have to do some personal research, and this can lead to some new information that you never would have looked into. Freelance copywriters see a wide variety of topics throughout their careers, and it might prove to be exciting.

- Traveling Isn't Required to Succeed: When you are doing freelance copywriting work, there is no need to even leave your house. Simply get on your computer and do what you need to do in the moment. Having a side job like this is great for those who are already feeling burnt out about their daily commute. You won't have to worry about being anywhere at a certain time. You'll only be responsible for the tasks that you choose to take on.

- Your Potential Is Unlimited: If you want to put a lot of time and effort into freelancing, you can. The amount of money that you earn is solely based on the ability that you put into the work. This is great for those who are looking for a way to earn money on the spot. If you are struggling with money for a few months, you can choose to take on some freelancing work. When you are okay financially, you will be able to ease up on your workload.

Cons:

- Getting Clients Can Be Challenging: It can be tough to get your momentum going with freelance copywriting. If you have never done the work before, you will likely not have any contacts to approach. You need to be bold and risk-taking if you want to succeed in this job. Reaching out to people is one of the very first things that you will need to do to get hired.

- You Will Be Turned Down: Learning how to accept no for an answer is something that you are going to have to get used to. As a freelancer, you aren't always going to get picked for the job. There are a wide variety of reasons for this, but you will need to let it go. Don't take your declinations personally. Instead, utilize them as motivation to apply for something else.

- Clients Might Get Difficult to Work With: Because you are going to be working with so many people at any given time, you might experience some personality clashes. In case you don't see eye-to-eye with your client, you need to be able to effectively express this. Creative differences can and do pop up, and this is normal.

- The Work Can Be Inconsistent: You might experience periods of time when you have an abundance of work to choose from. On the other hand, you will also experience times when the work is lacking. This is something to keep in mind when you get into freelance copywriting -- inconsistency can happen, but this is something you should know about from the beginning.

- No One Will Work For You if You Cannot: Working on your own terms offers many levels of freedom, but if you are experiencing an illness or emergency, remember that nobody else will be able to fill in for you. The same applies for times that you are feeling overwhelmed with anything else going on in your life. Just be sure to only take on what you comfortably can before you overwork yourself.

Create Success on the Side

Many people opt to have a side hustle in order to keep their finances on track, and with all of the different jobs that can be completed solely online, it is easy to see why. From ecommerce to freelancing, you can secure a job that will work around your life and around your existing schedule. Earning an additional income does involve effort, but it doesn't have to be a stressful experience. The goal is to make your life easier, not harder than it needs to be. With the financial gain, you will be even more motivated than ever to work on these simple tasks online.

Remember, you don't necessarily need another degree or training in order to work online. The main aspect that is required is self-discipline. If you are able to navigate through tasks and keep yourself in check, you will find success with any additional job that you decide to take on. A lot of people make the mistake of overloading themselves with two full-time jobs, but you don't need to! Having a side hustle means having something that doesn't need to be a main priority in your life.

You should be able to work your additional job when you decide that you need to earn an extra income, not when you are already drowning in tasks. This income might not even be a necessity, but rather, a security net for you to rely on when your main source of income is getting low. Having this extra way to obtain money is like having a bonus in your professional life. The best part is, you can do just about anything that you have a passion for. Businesses are always in need of extra help, so do some brainstorming to think about which industries you can see yourself being a part of.

Having an additional job means that you are able to multitask efficiently. By using these skills, you are also expanding your ability to learn new things at a quicker pace. This is important when you are approaching tasks on your own. You will also be thinking like an entrepreneur, deciding what steps must be taken in order to succeed. One day, your extra side hustle might have the opportunity to turn into something bigger. There is truly no downside, as long as you are willing to put in the effort that is required.

Take some time to think about what direction you can see your life going in; think about what excites you, interests you. This is a great way to get an idea of the type of online job that you should seek. The ideas presented in this guide were meant to teach you about some of your options. They are jobs that a lot of others have found great success in, but you are not limited to only these choices. Think about what job you can take on that would make you the happiest, and do some research while you plan your approach. Having the tenacity and the ability to keep trying will get you far in your career.

www.ingramcontent.com/pod-product-compliance
Lightning Source LLC
Chambersburg PA
CBHW081816200326
41597CB00023B/4273

* 9 7 8 1 9 1 3 4 7 0 0 8 1 *